Families and Faith

A Vision and Practice for Parish Ministry

Families & Faith

A Vision & Practice for Parish Leaders

LEIF KEHRWALD, Editor

TWENTY THIRD 23rd PUBLICATIONS

Contributing Authors

Judith Dunlap
Kathleen Finley
Jenny Friedman
Leif Kehrwald
Mariette Martineau
James Merhaut
Mary Jo Pedersen
Eugene C. Roehlkepartain

Twenty-Third Publications
A Division of Bayard
One Montauk Avenue, Suite 200
New London, CT 06320
(860) 437-3012 or (800) 321-0411
www.23rdpublications.com

ISBN-10: 1-58595-572-8
ISBN 978-1-58595-572-5
Library of Congress Catalog Card Number: 2005936955

Contents

Introduction

"Parents are the primary educators in the faith" (*General Directory for Catechesis*, #255). I would be surprised if you have not heard this statement, or similar sentiment, before. In my twenty-five plus years in faith formation ministry I have heard this statement used to motivate parents, and sometimes to berate them, with respect to their participation in and commitment to parish faith formation programs. I believe we have used this statement poorly and have misinterpreted whom the statement was written for. "Parents are the primary educators in the faith" was not written for parents and families, but rather for us, parish leaders. It was not written as an idealistic rallying cry, but rather as a point of fact. Quite simply, for good or ill, parents are the primary educators in the faith.

What if we truly believed that parents are the first and most formative educators in the faith? What would our faith formation programs look like? Would we continue to put such tremendous emphasis on child faith formation and such little effort toward parents and adults? Would we continue to conduct nearly all programs on the parish campus, giving only token energy to faith efforts at home? Would we continue to offer a "school-house" model of faith formation that separates children from the remainder of the faith community?

If parents are the primary educators, why aren't we seeking genuine partnership with them in our faith formation efforts?

Lifelong, Event-Centered, Intergenerational

I would also be surprised if you haven't heard the term "whole community catechesis." In recent years, leaders in Catholic faith formation have recognized the wisdom of the *General Directory for Catechesis* in stating that the community is "a source, *locus*, and means of catechesis. Concretely, the community becomes a visible place of faith-witness" (#158).

Faith formation is not just for children, but for everyone. Learning about one's faith and becoming a faith-filled person is a lifelong journey. There is no graduation, no exit strategy. Growing in faith is a communal activity and is done for the sake of the community. Each member has truth and insight to share regardless of his or her age, color, or sex. We learn from everyone, not just from those our age.

The GDC challenges parish leaders to explore the meaning and implications of lifelong catechesis for the whole community. In our work through the Generations of Faith project (see generationsoffaith.org), we have helped parishes adopt a vision and process for whole community catechesis that is:

- Lifelong—not just for children, but for everybody;
- Event-centered—utilizing a curriculum that emerges from the events of the life of the community through church year feasts and seasons, community events, and service and justice activities;
- Intergenerational—bringing all ages together to learn from one another.

If you are familiar with the vision and process of Generations of Faith then you know that we have developed a wealth of resources and tools to help parishes implement this vision. We have also produced many creative resources for families, at all stages of the life cycle, to engage in significant learning, discussion, and reflection at home. Why? Because we recognize the need for a strong partnership between the church of the parish and the church of the home.

Yet the presence of resources and strategies for using them does not automatically result in effective faith formation at home. Many parishes have developed wonderful home application resources, only to discover that some families fail to make use of the materials.

The pattern of behavior and the posture that the family takes toward the parish is strongly ingrained in many, many Catholic households throughout the country. What is that posture and pattern? It is a posture of passivity and a "drop off" pattern of behavior. While seldom expressed this way out loud, the prevailing attitude could be summed up in these words, "Here are my children. Please do unto them what you did unto me a generation ago."

I contend that church leadership over the last fifty to seventy-five years has fostered and reinforced this passive posture. For the past three generations we have communicated to families that the only faith formation worth its salt occurs on the parish campus (preferably in a classroom), facilitated by a trained expert and conducted through a highly structured educational model. The message has been: "We are the experts, so give us your children." The implied promise is that we will give back to them disciples, though the model doesn't seem to be working. Meanwhile, we confound parents all the more by periodically reminding them that they are the primary educators in the faith.

The chapters of this book seek to offer concrete ways to overcome the deeply ingrained passive posture, re-inculturate the home with Catholic identity, and in this way make it possible to have an effective partnership between the church of the home and the church of the parish.

A Vision of Partnership

We need to shift our focus on families from "objects" of our ministerial efforts to "partners." In her book *Family: The Forming Center*, Marjorie Thompson says it well, "What if family were not merely an object of the church's teaching mission, but one of the most basic units of the church's mission to the world?" (p. 26).

The church's vision of family is consistent with a vision of partnership. As is touched upon in several chapters of this book, the church's theology recognizes the family in a special ecclesial way. The *Catechism of the Catholic Church* states, "The Christian family constitutes a specific revelation and realization of ecclesial communion, and for this reason it can and should be called a *domestic church*" (#2204). The Christian family inherently contains all the necessary ingredients to be church.

Speaking directly to families, the U.S. bishops state, "As Christian families, you not only belong to the church, but your daily life is a true expression of the church" (*Follow the Way of Love*, p. 8). Just as the parish is an ecclesial unit, so too is the family. When the church of the home and the church of the parish work in partnership, then lasting faith formation occurs for all ages.

Yet, as you know, our practice in both the home and the parish does not always reflect the church's vision. Families find it difficult enough to talk about faith and religious practice, let alone actually share faith with one another. For a great many Catholics in North America, the home is no longer viewed as a center of religious activity. In addition, leadership in many parishes seems to have given up on the home and family. Something in their experience tells them that parish families won't really bother with the materials sent home. Before long, leadership stops the practice.

But there is more to it than just sending materials home. In this book—consistent with the vision of lifelong catechesis for the whole community—we contend that certain key elements of faith formation must occur at home. We simply must rekindle the family's desire, effort, and ability to be a center of religious activity. This doesn't mean they have to be perfect. They don't even have to "cover" all the material. Far more important are the intention and effort toward religious practice with people of all ages developing an ongoing pattern of practicing their faith at home, however imperfectly.

In his book *The Power of God at Home*, J. Bradley Wigger suggests seven specific practices:

1. prayer
2. sacred texts (reading aloud together)
3. meals
4. service
5. talk of God
6. celebration
7. building on strengths.

These activities, as you will read in Chapter Eight, correspond quite well with research that highlights certain key activities that have a direct influence on whether or not young people take their faith and religious practice with them when they launch into young adulthood.

Wigger offers these practices in the context of a broader discussion of the home as a key place where the art of religious practice must be rekindled. He reminds us of the value of practice not just for the sake of the forthcoming "performance," but for its own sake. One who is passionate about an activity—such as music, athletics, study—easily engages that passion while practicing.

When the home becomes an authentic center of faith expression, a true partnership with the parish not only becomes feasible, but does so with much less effort than we might imagine. When the parish community itself becomes the source, locus, and means for catechesis, then—to paraphrase Maria Harris—when the parish recognizes itself as *being* a faith formation program rather than simply *having* a faith formation program, then opportunities for the family and the home to contribute in meaningful ways abound.

About This Book

This book has been a group effort on the part of eight contributing authors, all of whom have a great deal of experience working in ministry with families, and each with significant expertise in their respective fields. (A short bio of the author is included at the beginning of each chapter.) Every chapter presents a different lens through which to understand the complexities of family life, and implications for faith formation in both the parish and the home. All eight of us have been working in some form of parish and family ministry for decades. We have made our share of mistakes, and we have each learned a great deal from the unsung heroes, like you, who continue in parish work.

This book serves as a companion to two other books that we at the Center for Ministry Development have written. These document the development of the Generations of Faith project (GOF):

- *Generations of Faith Resource Manual: Lifelong Faith Formation for the Whole Parish Community*, by John Roberto and Mariette Martineau;
- *Becoming a Church of Lifelong Learners: The Generations of Faith Sourcebook*, by John Roberto.

These two books—also published by Twenty-Third Publications— articulate the vision and break open the mechanics of implementing events-centered, lifelong, intergenerational faith formation in the parish. *Families and Faith* provides the necessary vision and some practical application for bringing the family and the home into partnership with the parish.

Unlike the two GOF resources, this book does not promote a particular set of steps and strategies for helping families grow in faith. It is not prescriptive. Rather, it is purposely designed to give the reader a myriad of ideas and strategies, some of which will hopefully be applicable to the reader's pastoral circumstance. Your parish need not be involved in Generations of Faith or whole community catechesis to benefit from this book. If your parish is comprised of families—what parish isn't?—then you will profit from using this book.

We have made a few assumptions about those who will read it.

As the subtitle states, this book attempts to articulate a vision and practice for parish ministry. As authors, we have assumed that the reader is a parish leader, whether volunteer or staff level, with at least some responsibility for, or influence over, one or more aspects of faith formation in the parish. These may include pastors, pastoral associates, youth ministers, directors of religious education, coordinators and team members for whole community catechesis, coordinators and team members for Generations of Faith, and other leaders. Yet this book is also appropriate for students enrolled in courses pertaining to religious education, faith formation, family ministry, and the like.

We assume the reader shares our belief in the holy and sacred nature of family living. Although several chapters (one, three, six, and eight) address the area in some detail, we do not offer a systematic articulation of the theology of marriage and family in order to convince the reader of this premise. For the time being, the words of the U.S. bishops in their 1994 pastoral message to families, *Follow the Way of Love*, will suffice:

> A family is our first community and most basic way in which the Lord gathers us, forms us, and acts in the world. The early Church expressed this truth by calling the Christian family a *domestic church* or *church of the home*....Your domestic church is not complete by itself, of course. It should be united with and supported by the parishes and other communities within the larger Church. (p. 8)

We assume the reader is aware of and has sensitivity to the vast diversity of family life that exists in parish life. Today's family is not what we were raised to believe it should be. The working father, stay-at-home mother, a couple of children, a pet, and a mini-van make up only a small minority of households in North America. In this book, the reader won't find statistical analysis of family configuration. We assume your experience in parish life has already formed your awareness that families come in all shapes, sizes, configurations, and colors.

Households are made up of a myriad of relationships, generations, and familial bonds. For the purposes of this book we draw a close link between the words "family" and "household," simply believing that God's gracious presence can be in any and every home. Many households that are comprised of "non-traditional" family relationships may not necessarily think of themselves as a "family." Yet we do consider them just that, and we assume you do, too.

This book is not the final word on families and faith formation. Rather, we prefer to see it as a discussion starter. While you read these pages, surely your own experience with families will generate strategies, concepts, even vision not articulated here. As those ideas well up in your mind, take a moment to sit with them, write them down, and implement them in your ministry setting. To the extent that you do that, this book has accomplished one of its most important goals. Never have we presumed that we hold the corner on all the possible ways to help families discover God's gracious activity in their lives.

As you read these pages you will also begin to notice some of the missing pieces. The most glaring of these is the lack of stated ethnic and cultural nuance and sensitivity of family life. It's not that we are not aware of the cultural and ethnic differences among families, but as a group of eight, we do not have the expertise, and to some extent the lived experience, to adequately address these concerns.

Also, given page limitations, the sheer complexity of exploring the varied cultural backgrounds from which our families come is not possible. In the limited spaced available we would be guilty of either being far too general to be helpful, or of leaving out far too many cultural and ethnic expressions. Obviously, there is an entire book on families and culture that must be brought to the field of parish ministry.

The reader can be assured, however, that the information and ideas presented here apply to families (and parishes) across cultural and ethnic lines. We believe this book can help you assist families of all shapes, sizes, configurations, and colors.

So let this work be a discussion starter rather than the final word. Read it. Discuss it with your colleagues. Engage families themselves in your thoughts and strategies. And if you wish, share your feedback with us, for we too are on a journey of lifelong learning. Send your comments directly to me, Leif Kehrwald, at lkehrwald@cmdnet.org. I will share them with the other authors.

About the Center for Ministry Development

Founded in 1978, the Center for Ministry Development is an independent, nonprofit organization whose core purpose is to bring the Good News in new ways to the people of God. CMD's mission is to empower faith communities and their leaders for effective ministry with youth, young adults, and families through ministry education and ministry development training, programs, and publications.

References

Catechism of the Catholic Church. Washington, DC: United States Catholic Conference, 1997.

Congregation for the Clergy. *General Directory for Catechesis*. Washington, DC: United States Catholic Conference, 1998.

Thompson, Marjorie. *Family, the Forming Center: A Vision of the Role of Family in Spiritual Formation*. Nashville,TN: Upper Room Books, 1996.

U.S. Catholic Bishops. *Follow the Way of Love*. Washington, DC: United States Catholic Conference, 1994.

Chapter One

Families & Faith Formation

James Merhaut

James Merhaut is a veteran religious educator, author, and speaker. He has worked on both the parish and diocesan levels in the areas of religious education and youth ministry. He currently works as an adjunct author for the Center for Ministry Development, regularly contributing family and intergenerational catechetical materials to the Generations of Faith Web site. He is a part-time director of religious education for St. Edward Parish in Youngstown, Ohio, and he is the author of Your Catholic Family: Simple Ways to Share the Faith at Home *(St. Anthony Messenger Press). Jim resides in Canfield, Ohio, with his wife, Debbie, and their five children.*

Editor's Note

Jim Merhaut starts us off with a clear and convincing vision for family faith formation. Pay attention to his definition and description of holiness, and the case he makes for the inherent sacred nature of family living. Jim challenges us to develop an understanding of holiness that is rooted in the incarnation in order to effectively help families grow in faith.

Family: A Path to Holiness

I had a conversation with a woman from my parish shortly after the death of Pope John Paul II. She told me how her Polish heritage gave her a sense of deep connection with the pope. She was visibly mourning his death, vacillating between tears of grief and tears of joy as she remembered the man who gave honor to her homeland. During the conversation she talked about how his great accomplishments made her feel a bit ashamed of her own insignificance: "He did so much, and I do so little."

I told her that I believe the pope would not want her to feel that way about her contribution. He would surely prefer to build her up and affirm the love that she shares with her husband, her two adolescent children, her parish, and her civic community. She is a normal mom and wife. She works hard to balance her family life with her community involvements. These are directly related to activities that her kids enjoy. She has always been dedicated to keeping her family active in our parish catechetical programs, and she is a regular volunteer herself. Her life, like the lives of most dedicated parents and spouses, and unlike the life of the pope, will probably go unnoticed by most of the world.

I pondered her life and our conversation about the pope for some time. I wondered—as I have many times before—how many more centuries must pass before the mundane realities of family life will be perceived by most people as paths to holiness. What is the family path to holiness and how can parish leaders help families find and stay on this path?

The family way of holiness can be understood as the foundational way to holiness. Faith formation in families leads to our first experience of holiness, and it is often the reference point for other systems of holiness. Kathleen Chesto has pointed out how the monastic prayers of the Divine Office mirror the feeding patterns of nursing infants. Traditionally, members of religious orders stopped what they were doing, whether it was work or sleep, and came together for prayer in order to give and to take spiritual nourishment. They did this at 2:00 AM, 6:00 AM, 10:00 AM, 2:00 PM, 6:00 PM, and 10:00 PM—a pattern remarkably similar to the pattern young parents experience as they feed their infants. Which do you think came first, monastic schedules or baby-feeding routines?

The titles of Mother Superior, Father, Brother, Sister, and even Pope are all borrowed from family language. Families came first, and from families and their experiences the world's religions developed their structures and habits, whether consciously or not. Our Judeo-Christian tradition is deeply rooted in family stories beginning with the mythological stories of Adam and Eve and Noah. The stories about the call of Abraham and Sarah and their descendants mark the historical beginnings of the three great monotheistic religions: Judaism, Christianity, and Islam. Family is the primordial starting point for religion; it is the seedbed of holiness.

Holiness in the human experience achieved its highest moment with the mystery of the incarnation: God becoming flesh in the person of

Jesus. The incarnation is also set in the context of a family tale: a story of Jewish betrothal, suspicious conception, public shame, and courageous love. The hidden years of Jesus' life, the growing-up years about which we know so little, were years spent absorbing the mysteries of family love and family life. We have every reason to believe that Jesus grew up in a normal, first-century, Jewish family. When he broke out into his public ministry, it was somewhat of a surprise to his family, friends, and neighbors. The gospel of Mark records that Jesus' family believed that he had lost his mind. His neighbors found themselves asking, "Is this not the carpenter's son?" Jesus was one of them, one of the "little people." There are no historically verifiable records of him or his family doing anything spectacular while he was being raised by Mary and Joseph in the small village of Nazareth. He was a regular guy.

But our faith tells us that this was no ordinary family, even though they didn't appear to be anything special to their contemporaries. This was a holy family, *the* holy family. And now that Jesus, the incarnate God, had taken on the family experience, family life in general could never again be seen as anything less than holy. It had been touched and transformed by the incarnate presence of God. Family and holiness are forever intertwined.

So what do we mean when we speak of family holiness? How does family faith formation lead to holiness? To answer these questions, we will first address the issue of what it means to be holy, then move on to a discussion of family holiness. We will close with a discussion of faith formation in the family as a path to holiness, and explore ways in which parish leaders can guide the family along the path to holiness.

Holiness as Separation

Holiness means "to be set apart" or "separated." In the traditional, biblical understanding of holiness, something is considered holy when it is set apart from common usage and dedicated to the service of God. For example, the Holy of Holies, the part of the Old Testament temple that was off-limits to everyone except the high priest, was a room used for nothing other than worshiping the presence of God.

Thousands of years later, we continue to understand holy things as those that are set apart. The churches in which we worship each week are buildings that are set apart for religious ceremonies, places where we consciously and publicly dedicate our lives to God in ways that we do not in other places. Holy objects such as chalices, paschal candles, baptismal fonts, and altars are things that are used only for worship; they are set apart and dedicated to the service of God.

All of our understandings of holiness are rooted in the idea that God is holy. He, of course, is the holiest of all beings because God, as one who is not created, is completely separate from everything else insofar as everything else is created. God's existence is so far beyond our comprehension because it is not limited by time or space or anything else associated with created existence. It boggles our minds to wonder about the God who is before the beginning of time. We find ourselves silenced in awe when we approach thoughts about the eternal and timeless existence of God. We stretch our minds to the ends of the universe and wonder what it means to say that all we know lies within the universe, yet the universe continues to expand, and God is within and beyond it all. The existence of God is truly set apart from our existence. The ancient Israelites expressed God's complete separateness by calling him "Holy, Holy, Holy."

Physical Holiness

This understanding of holiness as separation is not without its difficulties. If the holiness of God is based upon his separateness from creation, then human holiness can also be understood as a separation from the created order. It does not require a major leap of the intellect to consider spiritual things as holy and to consider material things as evil if one uncritically accepts holiness as separateness. One could begin to believe that the holiest people are the ones who are the least earthly. It is conceivable that holiness could be understood as a flight from the material world. This very tendency, in fact, has plagued Christianity from the first century until today.

The incarnation is the great corrective to dualistic notions of holiness. Dualistic tendencies in the history of religion propose that matter is evil and spirit is good. Authentic Christianity, on the other hand, exalts the goodness of the created order so much so that one could not imagine a Christian proposing the idea that God became less holy because of the incarnation. It would indeed be a heresy to suggest that Jesus Christ is a less-than-holy version of God because he took on the experience of human physicality. Even though holiness means to be set apart or separated, and even though God is distinct from creation in that he is not a created physical being, it does not follow that God's holiness is rooted necessarily in separation from creation. God's holiness, rather, is rooted in absolute separateness from the fallen ways of creation.

While it is true that God is totally other than creation, it is also true that God is intimately connected to creation. This truth is highlighted by the Christian belief in the incarnation. Divine holiness, expressed in the person of Jesus Christ, means to be absolutely set apart *from* sin and set apart *for* love. Holiness is not distinction from creation and physicality; holiness is separating oneself from the ways of sin so as to live a distinguished life of love.

It follows that human holiness is also a way of engaging the world without getting caught up in the fallen ways of the world. To borrow from the words of the evangelist, it is living in the world but not being of the world. Human holiness is not a flight from worldly things; it is being set apart from sinful attachment to things so that one can relate to created things in a spirit of love and freedom.

A Shift in Perspective

Parish leaders need to develop a sense of holiness that is rooted in the incarnation in order to minister effectively to families. Family living is embodied living. Day to day, hour to hour, and minute to minute, family members literally brush up against each other and the world around them as they explore the depths of love in and through their fleshy experiences. In *Seasons of a Family's Life*, Wendy Wright describes the embodied nature of family spirituality in the following way:

> Family life…is an intensely embodied life. Bodies jostling bodies for a place at the dinner table, bodies intermingling to create new bodies, which then inhabit one and then are held, carried, nursed, tended, bathed, and fed; bodies kissed for "boo-boos"; bodies patiently accommodated as they age and fail; bodies whose proximity one longs for and whose absence inflicts pain; bodies that keep one awake by crowding into bed on a stormy childhood winter night or keep one awake long past curfew in a sultry adolescent summer; bodies that arrive unannounced for a fortnight's stay; bodies whose presence is required at holiday functions; bodies lithe and limber; bodies stiff and aching— the sacred realized in intense engagement with other bodies. (p. 56)

Parish leaders who tend to understand holiness as a quiet moment with God in an empty church, or a highly structured and neatly organized liturgical experience that seems sublime until a distraught child screams out for immediate attention, will have a very difficult time understanding holiness in a family setting. Any parish that wants to minister effectively to families must develop a leadership team that appreciates the physicality of family life and holiness. An exploration of the dynamics of family holiness will help parish leaders develop a vision of family faith formation.

Family Holiness

What separates Christian families from other families? What makes a Christian family holy or complete? It is not necessarily the organizations to which they belong, although holiness will require the rejection of some organizational affiliations. It is not necessarily the house in which they choose to live, although the choice of a house and a neighborhood may be significantly influenced by one's path to holiness. It is not necessarily the things they own or the food they eat or the entertainment they pursue, but these too can be influenced by a particular path to holiness. Rather, Christian families are set apart from other families because their love for Christ is the primary motivation for all that they are and all that they do.

Christian families set themselves apart from many of the dominant philosophical presuppositions of their surrounding culture because they freely choose to live in the love of Christ while maintaining a dynamic relationship with the surrounding culture. Christian families do not seek to escape the world by retreating into a false piety; rather, they live intimately close to the world and engage it with the light of Christ as their guide, illuminating and celebrating that which is good and rooting out and rejecting that which is evil. Christian families are called to be prophets, witnesses to the power of God's love in the world.

On the outside, Christian families do not seem to be different from other families. Their clothes don't appear to be any different, but they are careful not to rely on brand-name clothing to communicate their worth to the world. They are set apart from the idea that wearing fashionable clothing determines or reinforces a person's place in the community. The same could be said of the cars they drive or the houses in which they live. Christian families do not rely on their possessions to determine their fundamental worth. "Therefore I tell you, do not worry about your life, what you will eat [or drink], or about your body, what you will wear. Is not life more than food, and the body more than clothing?"(Mt 6:25).

Holiness does not require that we be separated from possessions (although holiness *may* lead one to become remarkably detached from material possessions), but it does require a separation from greed and conspicuous consumption. The moderate and detached use of possessions is what separates the Christian family from families who espouse the ideas of materialism, consumerism, and unbridled capitalism.

Christian families acquire and use possessions in a holy way; they are not only to be set apart *from* being enslaved to their possessions but also to be set apart *for* the freedom of love. We are not free to love each other when we are preoccupied with our things. Preoccupation with our possessions leads us to be concerned about how our relationships with others will limit the fun we have with our things. Christian holiness calls families to be vigilant about the truth that people and relationships with people are more important than material possessions and the fun or entertainment that those possessions provide for us. My pastor often reminds the people of our parish that we are not put on this earth to be entertained; we are put on this earth to love.

Detachment from things does not mean that we cease to use or own things. Instead it transforms the way we use and own things by giving us room for freedom in our use and ownership. If I am not emotionally attached to my car, then I am free to allow my children, friend, or neighbor to borrow it when necessary. If I am not emotionally attached to my one acre lot, then it is a joy to share it with my neighbor's kids, and I can delight in my neighbor's creeping phlox that encroaches upon my side of the border. Detachment allows for freedom and a proper use of things, and because things are an essential part of family living, parish leaders need to help families to relate to things in a proper and freeing way.

I was sixteen years old when I was driving my dad's car to work on the snowy roads of western Pennsylvania. I lost control of the car as I was descending a hill and trying to negotiate a left turn. The back end of the car began to fishtail. I caught sight of a van, also out of control, coming over the next hill. The driver did what he could do to avoid hitting my car. In the split second I became aware that my driver's side door was going to collide with his front end, I remember thinking, "This is going to hurt!"

The next clear memory I have is being in the hospital with my parents at my bedside, expressing their concern for me. After a day or so with a pounding headache, I was fine, but my dad's car was not. It was totaled. I have no memory at all of my parents being more concerned about the car than they were about me. My parents were not wealthy (they were self-employed and raised nine children) and could not afford to absorb financial losses, but none of my siblings or I ever doubted that we were their prized possessions. The things that we had, few though they were, were expendable.

My parents were set apart from attachment to their car and set apart for loving their careless child (I was cited by the police for driving too fast under hazardous road conditions). They had every reason to be angry, but their love and concern for me overrode their right to punish me. The generous and holy love given to me by my parents continues to challenge and inspire me and my siblings to value people more than things as we mature in our adult lives.

Laura was a non-traditional college student at Slippery Rock University in Pennsylvania in the late 1980s and early 1990s. When my wife, Debbie, and I met her, Laura was living in her car and doing everything she could to finish her education after a failed marriage had left her with nothing. With the help of public assistance, some good friends, and her church, she eventually traded in her car for a simple apartment. She got a part-time job and continued to work on her education, but she could not save enough money to purchase a car to replace the one she had given up. My parents had recently given us an old car so that my wife could transport our kids while I was at work. How could we not share this car with Laura when she needed a vehicle to get her to meetings or other places that she had to be? It was a simple way that we could extend the love and generosity that our families had always shown to us. We were continuing the Christian tradition of holiness by putting the needs of people before our attachment to our possessions.

There is nothing spectacular in the examples of holiness that I have cited thus far. Parents forgiving their careless child and a young couple sharing a car with a friend in need are typical acts of love that happen all the time in our world. They are not holy actions or actions that are set apart because they are extraordinary; they are holy because they are set apart *from* selfishness and *for* compassion and generosity.

Family Faith Formation as a Path to Holiness

Holiness in families does not just happen. There is a path to holiness that families must choose to walk. It is a path that is sustained by the grace of God, yet it remains a path and therefore must be traversed with human effort. Family holiness is the result of a deliberate and conscious effort to respond affirmatively to the daily promptings of love that present themselves in the ordinary events of family living. Family holiness is saying yes to God whenever and wherever he calls in the midst of family relationships.

Family faith formation is as diverse as family experience. However, there are a few things that are common to all methods of family faith formation. In the limited scope of this essay, I will discuss the two common threads of silence and community support as necessary foundations for authentic family faith formation.

Silence

All paths to holiness begin with silence, and so it must be an essential part of family faith formation. God communicates directly to the human heart without the medium of language. Our language helps us become aware of God's presence within us, but in order to understand the silent language of God we must develop habits of silence in our daily lives.

God silently prompts the human heart at its deepest level and calls for a response of faith. Our response in faith takes us down the path to holiness. Silent moments with God give us the strength for holiness—the strength to be separated from selfishness and separated for love. It may seem strange to propose silence as the starting point for holiness in a family when families—especially in Western culture—are bombarded endlessly with noise. But because noise is so prevalent in our culture, perhaps silence needs to be the most deliberate effort of all in the development of family faith formation.

How can we encourage families to create space between the many noises of modern life without turning their homes into monasteries? There are a number of things that have worked in our home, but a word of warning is in order here. Just because a method of faith formation works for one family does not mean that the same method will work for all families. Each family must make its own path of faith formation in pursuit of family holiness, and it is essential for parish leaders to respect the diverse paths that families choose to travel. While it is helpful to learn about what other families are doing, and while some of the methods are transferable, others are not. Consider the following list as possible recommendations—or at least food for thought—to guide the families you serve:

- *Turn off the ringer on the phone during family meals.* This sends a clear signal that family conversation at mealtime is a priority. The noise of the ringing phone is an unnecessary distraction to family communion at mealtime.
- *Designate quiet space for homework.* If one child is doing homework in a particular space, all noise from electronic devices is banned from the homework space.
- *Encourage families not to give in to the temptation to accumulate televisions, stereo equipment, and other forms of electronic entertainment.* Is it really necessary for a family to have multiple televisions and stereos

in the house? To be honest, neither is truly a life necessity, but since most families have them it's important to discuss how to use them consciously and critically. Consider how having only one of each would not only cut down on noise, but also give family members the opportunity to practice negotiating skills when two or more disagree on what to watch or listen to.

- *On most days, one hour of viewing TV or listening to music is plenty.* Suggest to families that they set limits that are reasonable, and urge them to stick to these. In our family, our younger children were not permitted to have televisions or stereos in their bedrooms. These became a haven of silence. Entertainment and noise were reserved for the common family room.

- *Suggest that family members not go to sleep while listening to music or watching television.* Get into the habit of drifting off to sleep in silence with only the natural noises of your environment (whether rural or urban) accompanying the journey to slumber. If external noise from neighbors is too invasive, a fan from a heater or air conditioner is a helpful tool to cut down on the distracting external noise.

- *Discuss the necessity of "down time" for children.* Caution parents about overbooking their children's schedules with sports, lessons, social gatherings, and so on. Children of all ages need time and space just to chill out with the family.

- *Parents can encourage reading by making it a habit in their own lives.* They should also spend a little time each day reading to younger children. Regular trips to the public or church library are great ways to encourage reading and find silent places outside the home.

- *Encourage nature walks in local parks and preserves.* Suggest that parents comment on the splendor, diversity, creativity, and beauty of God's creation, but keep words to a minimum. Let the children explore and enjoy.

There are many opportunities for work that don't require a lot of mental focus, such as washing dishes, pulling weeds, doing laundry, cleaning floors, walking the dog, cleaning windows, and so on. We can look at these menial tasks as annoying disruptions to our otherwise interesting lives, or we can view them as opportunities for a bit of solitude and silence. Daily chores keep our hands busy while they permit our minds to be distracted. Unfortunately, many of us allow our minds to wander to things we would rather be doing, and that train of thought creates a sense of frustration as we feel trapped by our chores. But these chores are, in truth, little acts of love that we give to our families, and they should be considered nothing less than that. In the silence and solitude of daily chores we can become aware of God calling us to appreciate the loving nature of a chore.

As I do the dishes, I can become aware that it is love, which comes from God that motivates me to prepare clean dishes for my family to use at mealtimes. Some would say that my dish cleaning is undertaken only from a sense of duty; that is, I do it because I have to do it. But even a sense of duty is born from the love we have for another person. If I had no love, then I would be indifferent to the needs of others. I just wouldn't care, and I would do nothing for them. Imagine the filth and the disease that would happen if no one did the dishes! Washing dishes is not an insignificant act. It is an act pregnant with spiritual value. It's an act of love done in solitude and the silence of a wandering mind for the benefit of others.

The silence of the wandering mind of a person with busy hands deserves some attention here. Have you ever been busy with a simple chore while someone is talking to you, but you don't hear what is being said because your mind is off in another universe? This is a common human experience that reveals the mental power we have to silence the world outside of us while we withdraw from our surroundings into a world within. This mental power needs to be used carefully. It would not be wise to withdraw mentally while hiking along a narrow ledge in the Grand Canyon! But, in the right context, this mental power is an excellent way to create silence in the midst of a noisy household.

If parents can be encouraged to accept chore time as a gift, an opportunity to withdraw into the world within, then they can be taught to use chore time for silent prayer time as well. We can teach parents to reflect on the beauty of their daily acts of love. They can whisper a thank you to God for the grace of the moment that has freed them from the resentment they usually feel when they have to do chores.

To achieve this level of reflection, parents will need to be taught. Will you instruct them? They can pray a blessing upon the family members who will benefit from the work of their chores. Will you teach them to silently bless? Parents can pay attention to and take delight in the development of the small bit of beauty that their work creates in the home. Unfortunately, many parents miss these opportunities to commune with

God on a daily basis because no one has praised the sacred beauty of their household work. Will you praise them and their daily duties? This perspective can transform a parent's experience of doing chores. Will you help them to change their outlook so that they can discern the silent presence of God calling to them every day? Parish leaders can provide a great service to families by helping them to see the deep spiritual value in these simple acts of love.

Community Support

Now we turn to a more discursive foundation for family faith formation: the supportive community. Parish leaders are a critical part of the supportive community that helps families understand the dynamics of spirituality and faith formation in their daily lives. There are many important players in the development of a supportive community for families, but the parish leader holds a privileged role in community development. We will flesh out this topic more completely while we explore community support as a key to family holiness.

All paths to holiness must be supported by a caring and diverse community. Community, of course, begins with the loving and supportive relationships that families experience within the walls of their homes. But even for families that support one another and choose a path to holiness, it is very difficult to stay on that path if there are no external support structures. Families first need support from each other, but beyond that they need help from neighbors, the civic community, and their parish church in order to stay on the path to holiness.

There is a growing body of research that suggests many of our social problems are related to the fact that we, as a culture, have become very private. Kids left to themselves tend to become anti-social. How unfortunate are the stories of children bringing guns to school and shooting their teachers and classmates, leaving a community perplexed and distraught over an event that seemed to come out of nowhere. Unfortunately, that's the point because these kids really do come out of nowhere: they have no place to fit in. They are cut off from the community that has become too private and too exclusive, and the lost kids, with a depth of rage that is hard to fathom, turn on the community that has betrayed them.

The Search Institute in Minneapolis has an abundance of research that shows how beneficial social relationships can be in helping young people grow safely through adolescence and into adulthood. Neighbors who take the time to learn the names of the kids in their neighborhood are doing more than being nice; they are actually fighting crime. Giving a child or a teen a personal sense of belonging to a community is critical to absorbing that youngster into the community as a productive, peaceful member.

The high school in our community assigns every child to a teacher who will be that student's homeroom teacher for all four years of high school. Homeroom time is then periodically extended for the purpose of fostering the relationships between students and teachers. This is a simple way to make sure that no child goes through the system unnoticed. Each student is known by at least one teacher. It's not going to solve all of our educational problems, but it is a step in the right direction. It acknowledges that relationships are foundational to learning.

Civic communities can foster a deeper sense of belonging by encouraging interaction among citizens. A good network of sidewalks and hiking/biking trails can slow down the pace of a community by encouraging the more personal modes of transportation. Community events staffed by large corps of volunteers are a great way to help people to get to know each other. Too often, local leaders are more focused on the city budget than on the relationships that the budget serves. A healthy community will put people first and do whatever is necessary to encourage positive and regular interaction among citizens.

When neighborhoods, schools, and civic communities in general recognize that relationships are foundational to a healthy and productive society, they discover the fertile partnership with families that we as church leaders want to foster. Family is the primary place where relationship skills are learned. Societies that value social relationships over and above other things, such as economic advancement and academic achievement, give due respect to the family as the core of society. The family is the building block of society because of its relational focus. Many social ills can be traced to a lack of relational commitment in families. The *Catechism of the Catholic Church* recognizes the family as the foundation of society:

> The family is the *original cell of social life*. It is the natural society in which husband and wife are called to give themselves in love and in the gift of life. Authority, stability, and a life of relationships within the family constitute the foundations for freedom, security, and fraternity within society. The family is the community in which, from childhood, one can learn moral values, begin to honor God, and make good use of freedom. Family life is an initiation into life in society. (#2207)

Because of the essential connection between family stability and social stability, parish leaders need to encourage a relational perspective in society. When neighbors, schools, and other civic organizations value anything more than relationships, an environment develops that is hostile to the essential nature of family life. On the contrary, a strong relational perspective in society will provide a supportive context within which families can flourish; such a perspective will give families the confidence they need to be what they are called to be; that is, a place where love reigns supreme.

How can parish leaders be catalysts for developing the essential network of supportive relationships, both inside and outside of the family structure?

1. *Get into the home.* While it is not practical to spend significant amounts of time in the homes of all parishioners, there are other ways to get into the homes of your parishioners. First of all, parish leaders can develop a deeper understanding of the dynamics of family life by taking advantage of local course offerings from social service agencies or diocesan family life offices. There is little doubt that the church in particular and society in general go the way of the family. It is the basic social unit upon which society and the church are built, and no one can serve society or the church effectively without a solid understanding of what is going on in families.

The knowledge that parish leaders gain about family life will enhance their ministry not only because they will begin to understand the roots of their parish's problems and successes, but also because they will be more credible ministers. Families intuitively know when parish leaders genuinely understand their lives, and they can also tell when someone is paying lip service to their ministry needs.

Another way to get into the home is to provide families with the resources they need to enhance faith sharing at home. Every year there are more and more excellent family resources available from Catholic publishers to help parents to fulfill their role as the primary catechists of their children. Many programs and resources have helped families to enhance their ability to share faith, and some even encourage formal catechetical experiences in the home.

Formal catechesis in the home is doable, but it will not look much like the formal catechetical programs in parish or school buildings. In order for parents to get into the habit of formally catechizing their children without turning their homes into institutional classrooms, they will need much support from parish leaders to first become comfortable with their own understanding of their faith, and then to learn how to take advantage of opportune moments within the natural rhythms of family life to offer catechetical instruction to their children.

This highlights the absolute necessity for parishes to place adult catechesis as the top catechetical priority of the parish. A solid adult catechetical program in a parish will empower parish leaders to release the deep catechetical riches of parenthood. Adult catechesis for parents should not only offer a systematic presentation of Catholic doctrine, but it should also teach parents methods for home catechesis that are rooted in the natural rhythms of family life.

The family has a pedagogy of its own that has worked wonderfully for millions of years; we should be very careful not to impose classroom methods upon the family.

2. *Teach neighborhood skills.* Americans are among the most individualistic people on the planet. Clearly, we need to learn how to relate to each other, and it's a mistake to assume that common sense will solve our social relationship problems. Family holiness calls families to reach out beyond themselves to their neighbors. Parish leaders can be proactive in teaching people how to love their next door neighbors first and then their neighbors beyond.

Loving our neighbors begins with learning their names. Catholics need to be reminded by pastoral ministers to connect with each other in the neighborhoods. Simple gestures such as calling each other by name and smiling as we pass one another on our streets or see one another across our hedges are beautiful ways to show that we care about each other. A greeting and a smile tell others that we know who they are and we appreciate their presence in our life. It is a basic human need to be known and appreciated. Neighborhoods are built up and made more beautiful and more peaceful by those who take the time to interact in simple, personal ways.

We also know that there are common issues that cause division. Neighbors tend to fight over issues such as noise from parties or loud music, trees that extend across a border, locations of parked cars, physical appearance of property, and so on. Parish leaders could easily design catechetical sessions around the Christian mandate to love your neighbor, showing possible ways to address these divisive issues when they crop up. These real family issues that can be points of departure for holiness if families can find it within themselves to make choices that are motivated by love of neighbor. Faith formation in families will be much more effective for families that live in strong, unified neighborhoods.

3. *Build a network of civic relationships.* Government (local, state, and federal), schools, ministerial associations, and other civic organizations are important resources for building an environment that is conducive to family faith formation. The church is not an island unto itself. Its members have many social and civic obligations and associations. Society is a sum of myriad dynamic interactions between widely diverse groups of people. The church is one part of society in a certain sense, yet, as the herald of the kingdom of God, the church is, in another sense, the pacesetter for society. The kingdom of God is the source and goal of society. Parish leaders are in a privileged situation because they are part of society while being connected to a body that transcends society.

Effective parish leaders keep abreast of social trends and developments, spurred on by the activities of civic organizations, in order to offer guidance to families in their quest for holiness. Families are bombarded every day with choices that are presented to them from various groups, such as political organizations, telemarketers, fundamentalist evangelists, sports and leisure organizations, school groups, and so on. The Internet has compounded this situation in a radical way. The church has a responsibility to dialogue with and even guide society in such a manner that it will operate in ways that are respectful of the sanctity and integrity of family life. Parish leaders should not stand by silently while their parishioners are victimized by some of these organizations. We need to develop ways of interacting with key social players such as government leaders, school administrators, business organizations, and other groups to advocate on behalf of families.

At the same time, families need to take responsibility for social and economic participation in their communities. Parishes that integrate media literacy training into their catechetical program provide an excellent service to families. Parents and children need to hear the strong voice of the church as they sift through the virtually endless stream of advertising that comes their way. Parishes should regularly provide a Christian critique of contemporary media and advertising.

One simple way to accomplish this task is to provide table discussion guides that can be used in the home. These guides could provide Catholic discussion starters on popular TV shows, Web sites, movies, songs, products on the market, or even on more local experiences such as school trends, fairs/carnivals, community projects, community organizations/movements, celebrity careers with a local connection, etc. Parishes have the unique opportunity to provide this service to families because parishes are the church's way of being engaged locally. No other level of the church—for example, the diocesan office or the Roman curia—has the perspective to speak with authority regarding the local flavor of family issues in a particular community.

Parish leaders who take the time to understand the day-to-day reality of family living in their particular community will be more apt to find effective and truly meaningful ways to serve families.

4. *Develop and maintain a family perspective in your ministry programs.* American individualism challenges the very heart of a Trinitarian faith. Human beings are social by nature because we are created in the image of a Trinitarian God. Parish ministers who fail to honor this truth cannot be effective heralds of the kingdom of God. Each person who walks into our churches carries all of the relationships that have contributed to his or her life. We need to be aware of these relationships in order to know the person who stands before us. Knowledge of the people we serve is a key to ministry success.

Catechetical programs for children, whether school based or parish based, are not effective without a strong adult faith community and the full and active involvement of parents. Many parishes will need a complete revitalization of their catechetical program in order to bring adults back to the center of catechetical ministry and to honor parents as primary catechists. The church's catechetical documents have consistently called us to this adult perspective for decades; the time is now ripe for implementation through use of the many excellent resources available for family and intergenerational catechesis.

Conclusion

Family holiness is a critical part of vibrant church life and social stability. Parish leaders need to foster in themselves an incarnational spirituality and a broad social perspective in order to understand the nature of family life and family holiness, a holiness that sets families apart from selfish influences in society and sets them apart for loving relationships that can build a society consistent with the beauty of the kingdom of God.

Nurturing silent, reflective experiences of God in the midst of daily life and building a strong network of social relationships are two keys to creating an environment in which family faith formation can thrive. Families also need to be taught how to recognize the sacredness of their daily experiences.

Finally, all ministry programs in parishes benefit from a family perspective, one that does not treat people as isolated individuals, but rather recognizes the essential communal nature of human existence. Family faith formation, guided by pastoral leaders with a broad vision of community, promises to provide a bountiful harvest of vibrant parish life and peaceful social relationships.

Reflection Questions

1. Do you find it difficult to see family life as holy? Why or why not?
2. Silent moments with God give us the strength for holiness, the strength to be separated *from* selfishness and *for* love. How do you help families build silence into their lives? How do you nurture silence in *your* home?
3. How can your parish community encourage relationships between families, parishes, neighborhoods, schools, and other civic organizations?

References

Catechism of the Catholic Church. Washington, DC: United States Catholic Conference, 1997.

Chesto, Kathleen O. *Holiness FamilyStyle: More Family Spirituality.* Liguori, MO: Liguori Publications videocassette.

Wright, Wendy. *Seasons of a Family's Life: Cultivating the Contemplative Spirit at Home.* San Francisco: Jossey-Bass, 2003.

Chapter Two

Families Through the Life Cycle

Leif Kehrwald

Leif Kehrwald has worked in family ministry and faith formation on the parish, diocesan, and national levels for over twenty-five years. He currently serves as Project Coordinator for Family and Intergenerational Services for the Center for Ministry Development. Leif has published several books and numerous articles on family life, family ministry, marriage, and youth ministry. His latest book is Youth Ministry and Parents: Secrets for a Successful Partnership *(Saint Mary's Press). Leif has taught courses on family ministry, parish partnership, and family spirituality at Loyola University (Chicago), University of Dayton, and Mount Angel Seminary in Oregon. Leif and his wife, Rene, have two young adult sons and live in Portland, Oregon.*

EDITOR'S NOTE

Jim Merhaut concludes the previous chapter with several practical challenges for helping families grow in faith, including the development of a strong family perspective in all parish programs and ministries. One important factor for developing that family perspective lies in a good understanding of the ways families change and grow as they cycle through the stages of life. This chapter gives a snapshot of the developmental stages of family life, and illustrates the needs of families during different periods of their lives.

One of the constant predictors about family life is *change*. All families experience change, transition, and growth. Some of these changes can be predicted, while others are unexpected. This chapter covers the stages of the family life cycle. While every family is unique, and no family is utterly predictable, there are experiences of transition and growth that nearly every family wrestles with. These stages are not difficult to discern. This is how we name them:

1. young adult (unattached)
2. early married
3. family with young children
4. family with adolescent(s)
5. launching family
6. family in later life.

At each stage, the family must negotiate a couple of key developmental tasks in order to successfully transition from the previous stage. For example, in order for a newly married couple to transition into becoming a family with young children, they must develop their roles and skills as parents, and figure out how to maintain their own relationship while caring for a dependent child.

Each stage of family life presents its own challenges, which tend to nag at the natural human resistance to change. Although it takes time, eventually the family will usually find a comfort zone in the new stage. But lookout! Before long it is time for them to begin negotiating the transition into yet another stage.

Why is this important to the parish leader? Quite simply, families at different stages of life have different needs. If a parish leader can better understand the developmental tasks and struggles of a family, then he or she can be more pastorally sensitive in the ways that family may be expected to participate in certain programs and services of the parish. Also, as families negotiate their changes and transitions, opportunities for faith growth often open up. There is evidence showing that when parishes and congregations help families negotiate their change issues, families tend to become more inquisitive about issues related to faith and spirituality. Many of these change moments correspond with sacramental moments and sacramental preparation, so many opportunities are built into the structure of our religious practice.

As you read about the life cycle stages below, think about the families with whom you work and to whom you minister. Bring to mind some of the parents and children whom you know, and who represent the tasks and issues described. Also, keep in mind the following ideas:

Developmental tasks are not problems. Families develop problems of dysfunction when they are prevented from addressing the developmental tasks or choose not to do so. Events of trauma or significance, such as divorce, death, or long-term loss of employment, may disrupt a family's developmental process.

Developmental tasks don't go away. Even if a family's growth is disrupted, they must still wrestle with the tasks of the previous stage, even if at a later time. This can be more difficult because they are likely dealing with tasks related to another stage as well.

The oldest child usually blazes new developmental territory. Typically, the family grows and matures as the oldest child enters new phases and stages. Every new task for him or her is also new for the parents. When younger siblings deal with the same issues, they are no longer new and will likely not require the family to change in any significant way. Yet when there is a long age span from the oldest child to any of the younger children the family may have to deal with development tasks at more than one stage.

As a developing system, the family naturally resists change. Families prefer to "stay put" in the rules, roles, and responsibilities they have found to be comfortable. Of necessity, this creates a combination of health and sickness, function and dysfunction. Yet change must occur, and one sign of a family's well-being is their ability to recognize their natural resistance to change, and move beyond it to embrace a new stage.

Ritual can ease the pain of transition. One of the best ways that parishes can help families is to give them, and model for them, rituals that mark their transitions and growth. Parish leaders can give families and parents ways to celebrate key rites of passage for individuals and the family, such as the start of school for a child (first or last child), a daughter's first menses, high school graduation, "launch" of a young adult, and many other key moments of growth. When these times are ritualized and celebrated, the family gets to "try on" the new stage in a safe atmosphere and realize that it can work for them. The ritual also gives the family a marker in their page of history to which they can turn back and remember their moment of change. If the ritual is conducted within a community of support the pain of change is eased even further.

Some life cycle stages overlap from one generation to the next. For example, while the early generation is dealing with the issues related to the launching family—managing exits and entries in and out of the family system; renegotiating rules, roles, and responsibilities of family members—the later generation is addressing the tasks of an unattached young adult, dealing with questions related to life purpose and vocation, among other things. Also, it is not at all unusual for the parents in an adolescent family to find themselves sandwiched between their teens and their aging parents. Dealing with more than one stage simultaneously is stressful.

Think of the stages described on the following pages as a snapshot of a family at a given moment in which they exhibit the characteristics of family life at that stage. What is described is not intended to be a roadmap that each and every family will or should follow. The events of family living are much too varied and volatile to be that predictable.

Major events such as divorce, death, immigration, illness, and addiction can disrupt the family's journey through the life cycle. Even smaller or short-term traumas can cause the family to get "stuck" in a certain stage. Relocating to a new town, changing schools, changing employment, and experiencing other events can impact the developmental journey of the family.

Parish pastoral ministers must be aware of these major or minor events occurring in the family, *while also possessing* an understanding of the developmental tasks and issues families deal with at any given stage. Read through the stages. Bring to mind families you know, and consider some of the practical pastoral strategies listed for each stage.

Young Adult (Unattached)

Some argue that independent young adulthood does not constitute an actual stage in the family life cycle process. But when compared to past generations when the young person went directly from the home of his or her family of origin into the home of his or her spouse, today's young adults spend a significant portion of their lives "unattached."

During that period of five or ten or even fifteen years, the young adult is confronted with significant developmental tasks. These include accepting emotional and financial responsibility for himself or herself, formulating a personal life direction that may or may not be independent of family expectations, developing intimate and committed relationships, and establishing himself or herself in the work world.

Learning Needs
As the young adult addresses the developmental tasks mentioned, his or her faith formation needs to include the following:

- Having experiences of faith that are pragmatic, yet image-driven and technological.

- Creating opportunities to independently diagnose his or her faith needs in an atmosphere of dialogue and communal support.
- Taking opportunities to explore faith with peers.
- Exercising involvement and leadership in faith-building ventures. Young adults learn by leading and taking on responsibility.
- Experiencing support and appreciation of the older generation who respect them and give them a chance to share their gifts.

Parish Response

With these needs in mind, the parish community can support the faith development of the young adult by implementing some of the following ideas:

- Provide adult education resources and programs that help both young adults understand the dynamics of faith growth during the early stages of adulthood and that equip them for the task of helping one another grow in the Catholic faith.
- Offer special blessings or rituals at Sunday Eucharist for young adults who experience significant life moments, such as the first full-time job, a promotion, the purchase of a first home, and so on.
- Provide a prayer-of-the-day via e-mail to young adults.
- Offer reflection/retreat experiences for young adults on faith and spiritual themes appropriate to their stage of life.
- Provide educational programs that help young adults understand and equip themselves to handle the tasks specific to their stage of life, for example, refashioning family roles and relationships.
- When offering intergenerational programs, link single young adults with each other so they can be part of a "familial" group during the program.
- Encourage college students and other young adults to consider alternative vacation opportunities, such as third world immersion experiences, Habitat for Humanity, and so on.

Newly Married

Marriage joins not just two individuals (who may or may not have been married before), but also two families in a new relationship. Early marriage presents the new couple with a series of new challenges, such as defining and learning the roles of husband and wife; establishing new relationships as a couple with their families of origin and with their friends; and developing a commitment to a new family, with its own rules, roles, responsibilities, values, and traditions.

As they confront these challenges, the new couple often finds themselves reflecting on the influence of their family of origin (or previously formed family with another spouse) to draw insights, values, and traditions that they want to include in their new family. This reflection helps them to sort out emotionally what they will keep from the family of origin, what they will leave behind, and what they will create for themselves.

See Chapter Three for a more detailed exploration of the journey of marriage through the life cycle.

Learning Needs

As newly married couples address the developmental tasks mentioned, their faith formation needs include the following:

- Learning to pray as a couple. The couple should share their individual spirituality with one another in order to create a new spirituality for themselves as a couple.
- Choosing a worship community. They can either continue with a current community or choose a new one.
- Discerning interfaith issues. If the couple is a merger of two faith expressions, they must determine how to worship together and how to engage in religious practice together.
- Creating a pattern of family faith rituals. They must decide what rituals from their respective families they want to continue celebrating in their new home, and what new rituals they might add.
- Creating a pattern of learning about the faith. What will the couple explore together? What learning needs are specific to each spouse?
- Discerning a financial stewardship response. The couple must decide how they will practice charitable giving, and to whom they will give.
- Discerning a gift stewardship response. The couple must decide how to give of their time and talents in service to others.
- Nurturing their relationship. The couple must decide how to enrich their own marriage relationship on a regular basis.

Parish Response

With these needs in mind, the parish community can support the faith development of the new couple by implementing some of these ideas:

- Give each newly married couple a wooden memory box created by a group of parishioners. The box can include a Catholic family Bible, a copy of *Catholic Household Blessings and Prayers*, a journal, information about the parish, a blessing cup and accompanying prayers, Catholic/Christian art, a prayerbook for couples, and so on.

- Introduce newly married couples to the parish at Sunday liturgy.
- Each year, invite all couples married within the year to come together for a "refresher" on the sacramental nature of marriage. Ask them for feedback on what marriage looks like from the inside, compared to the outside, when they were in the midst of marriage preparation.
- Provide table prayers and discussion questions to use in celebrating anniversaries.
- Provide simple resources for couples to use together at home. These can serve as tools for learning how to pray spontaneously with one's spouse, finding styles of prayer that fit both of them, and so on.
- Offer ideas for a meeting between the two families of origin; provide tips and pointers to remember as two families meet.
- On the first five anniversaries, send new couples ideas for renewing their marriage commitment. Encourage them to pull out their marriage preparation materials, reviewing in particular their strengths and areas for growth. Suggest that they highlight one strength and area of growth to focus on over the next year.
- E-mail marriage tips to couples on a regular basis, inviting older couples to write the tips based on their experiences.

Family with Small Children

With the birth of a child, the parents embark on new life tasks: to accept a new member into the family, and to adjust existing rules, roles, responsibilities, and relationships to include the needs of the youngest members. One obvious challenge for families with small children is developing parenting roles and skills. Parents must negotiate with each other about how to accomplish a host of new tasks related to childrearing, not the least of which include household and financial concerns.

Parents must also realign their relationships with extended family to include roles related to grandparents, aunts, uncles, and cousins. As the children grow, the parents realize they must share the socialization of their children with others through child care, preschool, and other situations. These transitions point out the need for developing new patterns of family communication, traditions, and celebrations.

Learning Needs

As the young family addresses the developmental tasks mentioned, their faith formation needs include the following:

- Learning to pray as a family; creating patterns of prayer and ritual that the family undertakes together.
- Learning how to share faith and to talk about God in terms that a small child can grasp.
- Creating an atmosphere of faith in the home that includes valuing each other's experiences, introducing the wisdom of the community (Scripture and church teachings), creating an atmosphere of dialogue while seeing their family stories as connected to the stories of faith, and challenging one another to respond faithfully to God's invitation to relationship.
- Discerning and living out the values most important to the family and to their faith.
- Choosing paths of service that involve the gifts of the family.
- Continuing to keep the marriage as the prime focus of the family and thereby deepening its sacramental nature.

Parish Response

With these needs in mind, the parish community can support the faith development of the young family by implementing some of the following ideas:

- Create prayer partnerships and circles of support for families preparing for the baptism of a child. These can include parishioners who attend the baptism, who stay in contact by phone or visit after the baptism, and who share information about things going on in the parish that may interest and support the family.
- Invite groups of parishioners to create faith chests for each newly baptized child. The chest can include a Bible, resources for a home altar or prayer space (e.g., a cross, colored cloths for each season of the year), a list of children's story books, a book of stories about the saints, or a family prayer and blessings book. The faith chest can be as complicated as a home-built wooden chest or as simple as a purchased tote.
- Provide resources and programs that help parents understand the dynamics of faith growth during early childhood to equip them for the task of helping their children, and each other, grow in the Catholic faith.

- Provide households with resources to create a space for faith in the home: religious art, children's Bible and storybooks, stories of saints, and so on.
- Provide opportunities for parents to participate in learning with their children, and share ways to model faith for their children.
- Provide families with an annual family rituals calendar that gives them suggestions for simple rituals of prayer as they journey through the church year. Make it large enough to record their own events, and include seasonal rituals.
- Offer a special "re-entry" educational process and ritual to help families estranged from the church reconnect with the parish community as they celebrate the sacraments with their children.
- Provide families with a variety of prayers that include praise, thanksgiving, structure for spontaneous prayer, prayers of petition, and prayers of contrition.
- Host a parish family retreat.
- Give families tools and support to effectively communicate, solve conflict, and make decisions in age-appropriate ways.
- Provide or link families to parent education programs and resources that help them understand the developmental characteristics of their child and of the family at this stage of the family life cycle, and support them in developing the appropriate parenting skills.
- Provide an activity each month that will help families make a social justice contribution to your community: e.g., gathering canned food in their neighborhood, writing letters of advocacy, or purchasing clothing and toiletries for local shelters.

Family with Adolescent(s)

Adolescence ushers in a new era in family life brought on by new life tasks for the young person and the changing role of the parents in relationship to their adolescent children. The changes of adolescence— puberty, new ways of thinking, wider sphere of social activity and relationships, greater autonomy—present the entire family with a new set of challenges. In fact, it would be fair to say that the whole family experiences adolescence.

The challenge for families with adolescents involves allowing for the increasing independence of teens in the home, while maintaining enough structure to foster continued family cohesiveness and growth.

Adult family members, who are typically approaching midlife, are challenged to reflect on their own lives, in light of issues such as marriage, values, and career. Many families with adolescents also find themselves beginning the shift toward joint care for the older generation. As a result, patterns of family communication, traditions, and celebrations will all need adjustment.

The task for most families with adolescents—and it is by no means an easy one—is to maintain *emotional* involvement, in the form of concern and caring, while gradually moving toward a relationship characterized by greater *behavioral* autonomy.

Learning Needs

As families with adolescents address the developmental tasks mentioned, their faith formation needs include the following:

- Maintaining or creating patterns of prayer and ritual that coincide with the adolescents' often-expanded social and extracurricular activities.
- Reflecting together on changing patterns of family service; for example, an adolescent may now be performing service with peers rather than with the family.
- Integrating deeper questions about faith and church teachings into family conversation, as teens become more outspoken in the expression and understanding of their faith.
- Praying and sharing as fellow companions on the journey of life, as teens become more similar to adults than to children.
- Dealing with the challenges of society's values and norms as family boundaries expand to allow for greater autonomy of teens, who are now working, driving, and attending social functions on their own.
- Balancing individual spirituality with the spirituality of the family and of the couple.

Parish Response

With these needs in mind, the parish community can support the faith development of the adolescent family by implementing some of the following ideas:

- Provide resources and programs that help parents understand the dynamics of faith growth during adolescence and adulthood, and that equip them for the task of helping their teens grow in the Catholic faith.

- Offer resource materials for parents that are aimed at promoting family discussion of faith and moral issues, especially as they relate to the challenges faced by youth today.
- Organize parent-teen programs that enable family members to dialogue about common concerns: e.g., communication, morality, sexuality, and dating.
- Provide resources and/or programs that help families with adolescents create, revise, and celebrate a regular calendar of family rituals that reflects their family values and experiences, the practices of their family of origin, and the ethnic/cultural traditions of their extended families.
- Facilitate regular parish celebrations of milestones in the life of the family with adolescents: e.g., graduation from middle and high school, a first job, getting a driver's license, birthdays and sacramental anniversaries (baptism, first Eucharist, confirmation), promotions, job changes, and family moves.
- Celebrate as a community the rites of passage that mark the transition from childhood to adolescence; where appropriate the Orita or Quince Años celebrations can be adopted or adapted.
- Offer retreat experiences for family members—with themes appropriate to families with adolescents—organized in a variety of formats: e.g., parent-teen, mother-daughter, father-son, and so on.
- Model a variety of prayer formats, styles, and techniques in parish programs for younger and older adolescents.
- Provide for or link parents to education programs and resources that help them understand the developmental characteristics of the adolescent and of the family at this stage of the life cycle, and support them in developing the appropriate skills for parenting: e.g., communication, discipline, problem-solving, and negotiation.
- Involve the entire family in parish-wide efforts to assist those in need, and in programs aimed at changing the structures that perpetuate conditions such as poverty and homelessness.
- Provide opportunities for families to learn about issues such as ecology, hunger relief, homelessness, human rights, racism, and sexism, both on a local and on a global basis.

Launching Family

Families with young adults experience a significant number of exits and entries of family members. Grown children are launched into schooling, careers, and a home of their own. As young adults marry, their spouses and children become part of the family system.

One challenge for families with young adults is regrouping as a family when the young adult moves away from the family, and sometimes, moves back home. Grown children and their parents must re-establish their relationships to reflect adult-to-adult arrangements. Parents experience changes in their marital relationship now that parenting responsibilities are minimal. The whole family must realign relationships to include in-laws, grandchildren, and other extended family members. The parents may be caring for the older generation, and dealing with sickness, disability, and death.

Learning Needs

As young adult families address the developmental tasks mentioned, their faith formation needs include the following:

- Learning to share faith in adult-to-adult ways while giving young adults the freedom to shape their own adult spirituality.
- Celebrating family transition times with rituals and prayer, especially those transitions related to young adult passages.
- Dealing with death and illness of aging parents and grandparents; sharing beliefs about life and death with other family members.
- Learning as a family to embrace new practices of faith that speak to the life experience of the young adults within that family.
- Embracing interfaith or interchurch issues if the young adult develops a relationship with someone from another faith.

Parish Response

With these needs in mind, the parish community can support the faith development of the young adult family by implementing some of the following ideas:

- Incorporate topics of relevance to families with young adults into parish catechetical programs; for example, faith and midlife issues, spirituality of work, lifestyle decisions, marketplace morality, social justice issues, and sexuality.
- Offer intergenerational catechetical programs that enable young adults and their parents to gather as kindred groups or with families in other stages of life for faith learning and sharing.
- Develop and celebrate as a community rites of commitment to mark the young person's passage to adulthood and the decision to

participate in the life of the parish community in a new way.

- Provide age-appropriate resources and assistance to young adults and midlife adults (parents) that help establish their personal patterns of prayer.
- Offer Catholic prayer experiences for young adults and midlife adults (parents) in diverse spiritual traditions and practices.
- Provide young adults and their parents with the guidance needed to work through renegotiating their relationship as adult-to-adult.
- Publish a list of local counselors skilled in helping families at this stage in dealing creatively with the issues and tasks common to families with young adults.
- Provide a list of service opportunities for young adults and midlife adults (parents). Give young adults a reflection sheet or journal to connect the service experience to their Catholic faith after the service is completed.
- Offer opportunities for consciousness-raising and education on issues of concern both locally and globally: e.g., human rights, stewardship, and lifestyle.

Family in Later Life

Among the tasks of families in later life is the adjustment to retirement, which may not only create a vacuum for the retiring person, but may also put a strain on the marriage. Financial insecurity and dependence can also be problems, especially for family members who value independence and the ability to manage for themselves.

While loss of friends and relatives is a particular difficulty at this phase of life, the loss of a spouse is perhaps the most difficult adjustment. One must reorganize one's entire life to live as a single person, after living as a couple for many years. Grandparenthood, however, can provide opportunities for close relationships without the responsibilities of parenthood. This may also be an opportunity to become more involved in parish or community service, and establish new friendships.

Learning Needs

As families in later life address the developmental tasks mentioned, their faith formation needs include the following:

- Celebrating and recognizing God's presence throughout life.
- Searching for hope and meaning in the midst of loss and transition.

- Embracing the fullness of the paschal mystery: celebrating birth, life, suffering, death, letting go, and new life.
- Sharing faith and wisdom with one another and with younger generations.
- Exploring one's role as a disciple in the areas of justice and service.
- Wrestling with one's vocation as a baptized person who is in later life, and getting serious about the "whys" of life.

Parish Response

With these needs in mind, the parish community can support the faith development of the family in later life by implementing some of the following ideas:

- Prepare a rite of retirement that could include reflections on vocation across the life span, using people of Scripture such as Moses, Abraham, the prophets, and New Testament disciples. The rite could also feature reflections on vocation through examples from the lives of saints.
- Integrate healing events into parish activities; celebrate the Anointing of the Sick on the World Day of the Sick (February 11), highlight the lectionary readings on healing, and invite the parish to the annual Chrism Mass (Blessing of the Oils).
- Provide resources and programs that help adults in later life understand the dynamics of faith growth at this time in their lives. and that equip them for ongoing growth in faith.
- Host regular celebrations as a parish community to acknowledge milestones in the life of families in later life: e.g., career accomplishments and recognition, retirement, important events in the lives of children or grandchildren, or birthdays and sacramental anniversaries. Families can also be encouraged to mark these events with celebrations at home.
- Provide opportunities for families in later life to come together for prayer and support.
- Offer educational programs that help older adults and their families understand and handle the family tasks specific to families in later life: e.g., reassessing work and social commitments, grandparenting skills, and managing the relationships between adult children and older parents.
- Provide personnel and program resources to help family members deal with the death of a spouse or parent.

- Organize a respite care program to assist adult children who are caregivers to their parents.
- Provide service opportunities that allow older adults to share their work, technical, and professional skills with others.
- Help older adults serve as career mentors for young adults.

Conclusion

Understanding life cycle theory can give the parish minister a foundational understanding of what families are dealing with as they involve themselves in the life of the parish. Keep this information in the forefront of your thoughts as you plan your programs, and as you find yourself in pastoral encounters with families. You might make adjustments in the scheduling and format of your programs to take into account the developmental needs of families at each stage of the life cycle. You may want to implement or adapt some of the practical pastoral strategies listed in this chapter.

Reflection Questions

1. What difference might it make if a parish were to intentionally address the needs of families at each stage of the life cycle?
2. How do you or your parish currently address the needs of families at different stages of the family life cycle? On which stage of the life cycle does your parish focus the most attention? Which stages get less attention?

Chapter Three

Marriage Across the Life Cycle

Mary Jo Pedersen

Mary Jo Pedersen, M.A., is marriage and family spirituality resource person for the Family Life Office in the Archdiocese of Omaha, Nebraska. In addition to her diocesan work as Coordinator of family ministry training, she is an author and teacher and presents workshops and retreats nationally and internationally on topics related to marriage and family life, lay ministry, and faith development. Mary Jo has authored many books and resources for families as well as parish programs for faith development of couples and families. She has served as a lay advisor to the USCCB Committee on Marriage and Family and writes for Catholic News Service's Faith Alive series. She has been married for thirty-six years and has three grown children.

EDITOR'S NOTE

Just as families journey through certain somewhat predictable stages, so do couples—though the stages are not identical. As time marches on, relationships change and evolve. Spouses must make adjustments in the ways they interact with each in order to keep their marriage alive and growing. Even if you are not directly involved in marriage ministry, your understanding of their journey will undoubtedly help in your efforts at family faith formation.

When married couples enter the parish for an experience of learning, celebrating, and serving, they come as individuals who are connected to God and one another in a unique way. They bring with them an intricate web of relationships. Whether they enter the church alone or as a couple, their lived experience is shaped by their relationship with one another and

41

by the entire system of in-laws, siblings, parents, and perhaps children whose lives are inexorably bound up with theirs. The commandment to love God and neighbor and self begins in this intimate system of relationships and duties.

Before they enter the church or parish building, a couple's faith formation is taking place in the promises they made to be faithful in good times and in bad, in sickness and in health, until death. Whether they were aware of it or not, their pledge to love and honor one another was a radical statement of faith in one another, in God, and in the gathered community.

Everything they learned about their faith is practiced, tested, and celebrated in the shared life of the covenant they entered on their wedding day; this covenant is shaping and forming them each day by the demands of love. She has learned about forgiveness and practiced it when he forgot their anniversary. He is beginning to get a glimpse of what steadfast love means when he stands by her during the long illness of her mother. They have entered, often unknowingly, into the paschal mystery as they face letting go of dreams, such as going to graduate school, or having a bigger home, or raising the perfect child.

A shared, committed life can in itself be a source of grace. It teaches spouses patience, fortitude, compassion, humility, and kindness. A loving embrace provides a foretaste of the communion God desires with us.

Marriage is a school of unconditional love. Each spouse has the power to image God's love for the other in simple ways, such as providing a listening ear after a difficult day's work, or heroic ways, like supporting a spouse through rehabilitation after a stroke.

That same married life can be a source of temptation and alienation from God. A spouse's compulsion for neatness may lead the other to anger and retaliation. One may be obsessed with computers or race cars while the other responds by withholding affection. Lying, greed, resentment, infidelity, and selfishness can emerge from the close proximity of spouses as well.

Because married adults in the parish are being formed in their everyday lived experience of sacramental marriage, parish efforts to evangelize and catechize adults must take into consideration and build upon the unwritten catechism of marriage that exists within the home. For parishes to support and provide education for the vocation of marriage is to provide adult faith formation at the most immediate level of lived experience.

Baptism is a Christian's first and universal call to holiness, and marriage for most is the specific sacramental pathway to holiness through which they come to the knowledge and experience of God and the practices of Christian life. This chapter aims to provide a view of the developmental stages of marriage. The goal is to assist parish leaders to be aware of and build upon the opportunities for growth contained within the vocation of marriage as couples live a partnership of love and life.

The social sciences provide us with a fairly standard cross-cultural pattern of how a marriage relationship develops over time. A commonly accepted life cycle for marriage goes like this: first, courtship and marriage and the couple before children; second, couple's transition to parenthood and the childbearing years; third, marriage in the children's teen years; fourth, marriage as children leave home; and fifth, the later years of marriage as couples age. There are a variety of life cycle theories attributed to marriage; this one is simple and allows for a brief description of developmental tasks with an eye on how faith growth takes place over a lifetime of committed love.

The developmental cycle of marriage argues that at each stage of a couple's growth they must master a set of tasks that are specific to that stage and which, when mastered, enable them to go on successfully to the tasks of the next stage. Developmental tasks can be seen as challenges that lead to maturity and behavioral change for each spouse individually and for the "us" that is forming between them. The commonalities in adult development are lived out differently depending upon the particular cultural milieu in which one lives. One cultural formulation of the life cycle of marriage is descriptive of many couples, but that formulation does not predict what will happen from one year to the next for everyone. Couples move through the stages in diverse styles and at their own pace.

Though the basic elements of change and adjustment to age, task, and personal growth are common to all, there are important differences in the way some couples progress through the stages of growth. Later in the chapter, I will comment on those differences in ethnic families, divorced and remarried couples, and couples experiencing crisis.

Knowledge of life cycle stages is a helpful guide in the work of adult formation because it allows parish leaders to better understand the complex progress of adult growth going on in households of faith. It also assists leaders in building parish adult formation opportunities upon the lived experience of adults. Adults learn best when new information is connected to what they already know and is delivered at the best readiness moment.

The most important times for growth and conversion are times of transition between life stages. Personal experience and scientific research both reveal that times of transition, which are periods of significant upheaval in marriage, are key readiness moments for faith formation. These are moments when couples experience the loss of one thing and the gain of another. From a faith perspective, these are points of entry into the paschal mystery when adults experience in their daily lives the reality of dying and rising to new life. These times of change and transition can be evangelizing moments when community support and opportunities for reflection provide a meaningful context for growth in faith. By offering like-to-like ministry during times of transition or crises, parishes can effectively reach diverse households of faith.

Because faith growth is intricately tied up with a person's emotional, physical, and social growth, faith develops along the lines of an adult's lived experiences. For example, in the early years of marriage, spouses have the task of joining two lives into one household. Sam is beginning to learn that he has to put the needs and concerns of Sandy above his own in some circumstances. This practice of placing the other over self promotes growth in Christian life. Jesus is the model for selfless love, and the more one develops the ability to love this way, the more one grows in the image of Christ.

At every stage of development, there is an opportunity for the parish to make connections between faith and everyday life. When adult formation programs meet adults at their points of growth, and provide them with opportunities to reflect on their everyday experiences, challenges, joys, and losses in light of their faith, it moves them from seeing faith as merely a set of beliefs and practices to experiencing it as a lens through which all human experience is seen.

What follows is a brief look at five developmental stages of marriage, including a description of the challenges and tasks that lead to adult maturity, and some suggestions of how parishes can meet couples at each stage in a way that promotes adult faith formation.

Courtship and Marriage Before Children

Before the Wedding

What is going on?

Sam and Sandy sit close to one another at Mass, shoulders and hands touching. They notice things like the distance from the main aisle to the altar and the sound of the organ. They are planning their wedding and have entered the church's marriage preparation process. Like many young adults, they have not attended Mass regularly since leaving home, and are establishing a connection together for the first time with a parish church. They may not have had any religious instruction or opportunity for faith reflection since confirmation or graduation from high school. Sam has no formal religious affiliation but comes to church with Sandy who grew up Catholic.

What can the parish do?

Statistics show that a large percentage of couples like Sam and Sandy are coming to marriage preparation in the church without benefit of regular Mass attendance or formal membership in a parish. In addition, between one-third and one-half of Catholics marrying today are marrying non-Catholics, and so are bringing two faith traditions or one religious and one non-religious person to the sacrament of marriage. Therefore, when they come to the parish for marriage preparation, a welcoming posture is critically important.

- For interchurch couples a strong RCIA process is the doorway to a lifetime of adult formation for both spouses. If done well, it establishes both a learning relationship and an intimate social connection with parish community. Research shows that in 43.8% of interchurch marriages, one spouse converts to the other's religion (*Ministry to Interchurch Marriage: A National Study*, Center for Marriage and Family, Creighton University, www.creighton.edu/MarriageandFamily). Although many couples move away from the parish where the marriage took place, for those who stay, an organized follow-up process to the RCIA is a way of establishing a habit of adult formation across the life cycle.

- A well-designed and carefully executed marriage preparation program helps couples to see the parish as a place for adult growth. Marriage preparation is a key evangelizing and catechizing moment for couples. Both the process of preparation and the persons conducting it leave a lasting impression on those who approach the church at this joyful yet stressful time. Since eighty-five percent of Catholics marry at some point in their lives, marriage preparation and enrichment can be powerful adult formation for the vocation of marriage. In addition to a marital inventory and an educational program, such as Engaged Encounter, some parishes offer a blessing at Sunday Mass for engaged couples, and assign parish sponsor or mentor couples to the engaged as part of marriage preparation. Newlyweds often receive a family Bible, a subscription to a young married's newsletter, or another gift from the parish. These practical efforts establish the parish as a supportive learning environment at this time when a household is forming.

Some couples coming for marriage preparation may have been alienated by a member of the clergy or lay staff in the past, or they may have unreconciled issues with the church's teaching. These are significant issues for adult formation. Marriage preparation may not be a time to solve these problems, but it can be an experience of growth that opens adults to further explore and reconcile these issues at another time. Studies of marriage preparation in the Catholic church show that a team of clergy and trained lay people is the most effective combination for this ministry (see *Marriage Preparation in the Catholic Church: Getting It Right*, Center for Marriage and Family, Creighton University, 1995).

After the Wedding

What is going on?

Sam and Sandy still sit close together at Mass, though concerns about the church space have been replaced by worries about how they will get to the grocery store, clean the apartment, and have some free time together on this one flexible day in the work week. Though still regarded as the "honeymoon" period, this stage represents a radical shift from single to married life. Couples establish priorities regarding career, finances, lifestyle, time management, children, and relations with extended family. A new set of adult skills is being learned regarding patterns of communication, conflict resolution, and forgiveness. Couples often join individual spiritual beliefs and values, and they develop joint religious practices. Many newly married couples have substantial debts and are isolated from family and friends because they have been in transition due to education or work. The amount of time couples spend in this stage has dramatically increased in recent years. The newness of married love carries couples along in this period.

If the sacrament of baptism ("baptism" comes from the Greek word for "plunge") plunges believers into the life, death, and resurrection of Jesus Christ, then starting a marriage is a dip into the deep end! In terms of faith formation, this is a life stage in which the meaning of dying and rising can be understood in a new and profound way. Spouses are challenged to die to their former single life with its privacy, independence, and complete control of personal decisions. Now the two have become one "body," while retaining their own individuality. They now have the potential for a new life in a union that both signifies and brings about the love of God for his people. The couple is becoming a sacrament over time. Lessons in self-sacrifice, radical acceptance of one another (honoring), forgiveness, and unconditional love are part of the daily curriculum. Issues regarding sexuality and decisions about having children are inexorably bound up with religious beliefs.

Such decisions and negotiations are often regarded as simply psychological or emotional adjustments but, in reality, the daily demands and compromises are deeply spiritual practices. Sam and Sandy are being transformed. Values and beliefs are being tested. They need skills for communication and conflict resolution, and spiritual formation in the process of discernment. This is an exciting and vulnerable time for them individually and for their marriage. In a society that promotes individualism and autonomy, their sacramental marriage is countercultural; it calls them to a common life, the purpose of which is to build up the reign of God.

What can the parish do?
Because adults who stay married have chosen the countercultural lifestyle of committed marriage, they need the company, support, and encouragement of others who share this vision of marriage. The parish provides a font of grace for them through the sacraments, through the company of peers with similar beliefs, and through opportunities for continued growth in a lifestyle that is a call to holiness.

- One helpful thing a parish can do is to become a welcoming environment for adults without children. It is important to have young adults, both single and married, visibly involved in parish ministries. This takes some intentional pastoral practice since young adults are often "invisible" parishioners. A personal call is often necessary to invite service on the parish pastoral council, in liturgical ministry, or on other parish life committees. Some parishes provide non-competitive sports teams for couples, or make special pastoral efforts to contact them for projects such as Habitat for Humanity or service with the poor. Couples with no children, though they sometimes have challenging work schedules, frequently have more free time to donate to parish life if they feel needed and valued as full members.
- Young married groups provide a supportive environment and opportunities for social connection, service, and learning. In one sense, outreach to young married adults (and singles) is like the

missionary work of long ago. The most successful missionaries always introduced the gospel message as they addressed the needs of the people, including medical care, food, and safety, while they introduced the gospel. The same is true today. Most newly marrieds don't feel a strong need for Bible study. Their concerns are how to manage time, achieve a satisfying sex life, and negotiate money issues (see *Time, Sex, and Money: The First Five Years of Marriage*, Center for Marriage and Family, Creighton University, 2000). If the parish helps them address those issues in a practical way, it becomes a credible place for growth, and their faith becomes a framework for addressing the challenges of adult life.

- An ecumenical marriage group or inquiry classes can provide special assistance for interchurch couples, who have a higher rate of divorce than same-church couples. Research shows that marriages in which the couples have shared religious practices have greater longevity and satisfaction (see *Ministry to Interchurch Couples: A National Study*). Some non-Catholic spouses who cannot receive communion at Mass feel unwelcome in the parish. Ecumenical gatherings for these couples are essential to their ongoing faith formation.

- Intergenerational programs can also provide a network, perhaps even a safety net, for Sam and Sandy who are miles away from parents and extended family members at this time of transition to married life. Such learning opportunities assist in integrating couples without children into the parish structure.

- Many parishes offer marriage anniversary celebrations in which both the longest married couples and the most recently married couples are recognized, and all married couples receive an annual blessing. Such rituals reinforce the couple's confidence in their choice of sacramental marriage.

- As couples begin the process of family planning the church can offer education in the Catholic view of human sexuality as a holy dimension of human relationship that connects them to the creative power of God. Classes in fertility awareness and natural family planning provide a healthy countercultural view of sexuality in marriage, along with safe and healthy methods for planning for children.

- Most divorces in America today take place in the first five years of marriage. Divorce can be a devastating emotional and spiritual experience. Many who divorce feel like outcasts at church. Diocese and parish can work together to provide companionate pastoral care through programs such as the Beginning Experience program and coping sessions for divorced. Because most of this population will re-marry, healing the loss of a marriage is essential for the health and integrity of any future marriage. An effective outreach to the divorced is an indication that the adult formation program follows Jesus' command to care for those who are hurting and marginalized.

Couple Transition to Parenthood

What is going on?

Sam and Sandy have moved closer to the back of church and now sit separate as bookends for their child's infant seat and their squirming four-year-old twins. They are concerned about making it through Mass without an episode of crying, fussing, or emergency diaper change.

This phase brings with it the challenges of adapting to the role and duties of parenthood and negotiating the distribution of child care and household responsibilities. The joy of a new child is accompanied by the pressures of balancing career, parenting, and the need for spousal intimacy. With each child, time for private dialogue and couple intimacy decreases. These active and sometimes hectic years are often accompanied by increased costs of living, geographic mobility, the employment of both spouses, and in some cases, the death or illness of parents. All of these place pressure on the couple and require improved communication and negotiation skills, as well as support from others.

Couples must make important decisions regarding how many children they would like to have and how they will educate and care for them. These decisions affect lifestyle and career and have long-term emotional and spiritual repercussions.

Sam and Sandy invest themselves deeply in their children's growth and development. In this stage, the couple's interactions with others change. They are more open to developing relationships with institutions that serve their parenting needs and their children directly, such as child-care providers, pre-schools and schools, sports teams, and churches.

What can the parish do?

- When a couple brings their child to the church for baptism, they have the opportunity to reconsider what they believe and what they want to pass on to their child. The baptismal moment is another key evangelizing opportunity when the parish community can provide support and encouragement for the essential work of parenthood. For interchurch couples, this is another touch point for sharing faith traditions and establishing relationships with the church community. Many parishes seize this moment in the life cycle to provide adult formation regarding the history and theology of baptism. Some parents have had no sacramental catechesis since their teen years. Their baby's baptism is an occasion to reconsider their own baptismal vows in the context of their role as primary faith nurturers for their child. In the childbearing years, a faith community can provide the critical peer support that parents seek. Some baptismal programs offer couples a fresh look at the vocation of marriage and the deeply spiritual nature of parenthood as a call to holiness.

- Resources and information for couples regarding family planning and fertility awareness are an important aspect of the spiritual formation of adults at this life stage. The vocation of parenthood brings with it the privilege of becoming co-creators with God. Childrearing is a significant dimension of each parent's call to discipleship. Programs and resources that help couples make positive decisions to serve and nurture life are a crucial part of their adult formation in faith.

- Marriage education and enrichment programs help couples in this life stage continue their growth in faith by strengthening their commitment to marriage. Their call to discipleship comes in a fundamental way within the intricate web of relationships of their domestic church, moving from there into the larger church and community. The pressing needs of children and their many activities leave little energy for parents to concentrate on personal faith growth. Parishes can promote programs that focus on faith as a framework for coping with the everyday challenges of marriage and family living.

Parenting Adolescents

What is going on?

Sam and Sandy slip into the pew a bit late, a disheveled seven-year-old in hand and the teen twins reluctantly dragging behind. Disagreements about what to wear to church cause them to arrive distracted. Their concerns have turned to the choice of high schools for the twins and the increased cost of raising adolescents. If they choose a Catholic school,

Sandy will have to return to work, but she has been unable to find part-time work that would allow her to be home when the children return from school.

Like many couples at this stage, Sam and Sandy are faced with the double challenges of responding to the demands of adolescent parenting and wrestling with their own midlife issues. A teen's task of separating from parents demands flexibility and a constant effort to balance their children's increasing freedoms with firm limits.

Though separating from parents is a lifelong task, in adolescence it demands more compromise and negotiation than at any other time.

Conflicts with teens can negatively affect the marital relationship, especially when one parent tends to be more rigid and the other more flexible in dealing with rules and limitations. The adolescent's drive for autonomy and independence challenges the parents' ideas, values, and beliefs. Studies of marital satisfaction over the life cycle consistently show that marital happiness decreases markedly during these years. Marriages are at risk in this stage because couples have less opportunity for time alone, less confidence in their ability to parent, greater financial challenges, and increased concern about their own careers.

Another stress-producing factor can be the adolescent's struggle with sexuality and with school life, triggering the parents' own midlife issues regarding sex and work. Parents often feel uncomfortable talking with their children and teens about sex because their own parents never talked openly about it. Blended families are particularly vulnerable to distress when the couple is in their early adjustment stage and their teen children are challenging their authority.

Adolescents move through this stage in their unique way; some are belligerent and angry in their differentiating from parents, and others are withdrawn and passive.

Not all parents of teens experience serious midlife issues. But most adults at this stage of life are asking personal questions with some degree of intensity: Is my work meaningful? Will I reach my career goals? Am I a good parent? Will my kids do well in life? Did I marry the right person? Since religious beliefs often underpin life issues, asking these questions—either consciously or unconsciously—opens up an opportunity for adult growth in faith.

What can the parish do?
It's important not to assume that all marriages in this stage are in crisis.

There are many rewards in watching children grow and mature, yet most adults have some of the above concerns. Some helpful parish responses include:

- Providing opportunities for midlife marriage education and support. Current research indicates that strong and healthy marriages make for better parents and reduced stress between parent and child in the adolescent years. Kids try to play parents against each other, further undermining parents' authority and increasing teen anxiety and couple conflict. Parents who sharpen communication and negotiation skills and understand adolescent development will be more effective and less conflicted when speaking with their child.

- Offering counseling for couples and families who are experiencing difficulties. This can be accomplished either by referral to trusted therapists, or by providing part-time counselors with sliding scale fees on parish staff. Information on available counseling services should be easily accessible and in plain sight in the church environs. This takes some of the stigma away from seeking help, and sends the message that the parish cares about the emotional and psychological health of its members since it is inexorably bound up with their spiritual health.

Launching Young Adults and the Post-parenting Years

What is going on?

Sam and Sandy come to church alone, arriving early. One of the twins is married, while the other, who is still single, is completing an apprenticeship in a local plumbing business. Their concerns revolve around their daughter-in-law's pregnancy and the long battle of Sam's mother with cancer.

Sam and Sandy are experiencing the changes that come with launching children. This stage is a relatively recent development and a lengthy stage for some couples due to longer life expectancy and couples' having fewer children. The challenges to adult growth and maturity, though they vary with economics and ethnic factors, are basically the same for most couples.

First, they are becoming reacquainted as a couple. Their lives no longer revolve around children's activities, and they are making efforts to find new ways of being a couple. For Sam and Sandy, this is a happy time bringing increased marital satisfaction and intimacy, but for many couples who have drifted apart during the hectic childrearing years it is a crisis that often leads to a marital stalemate.

Second, they are redefining their relationships with their children from parent-child to adult-adult.

Third, their family is expanding to include in-laws and grandchildren.

Fourth, they have assumed new roles as caregivers to their aging parents. For Sam, this experience has become an opportunity to resolve a troubled relationship with his parents.

There are no hard and fast markers for couples entering or exiting this phase. For many reasons, what used to be called the "empty nest" is now referred to as the "revolving door" stage. This description refers to having adult children moving back into their parents' home for periods of time due to unemployment, delayed marriages, divorce, or pregnancies outside of marriage.

This can be a period of fruition and great satisfaction for couples or a time of frustration over failures in childrearing, work, or intimate relationships. For adults maturing in faith, the spiritual tasks of this stage are aligned with the most profound mysteries of the faith tradition. Though the rewards can be great, the losses are also significant. Sandy's mother had a serious stroke and needed assistance for a year before she died. At the same time, Sandy is letting go of her son who is marrying and moving away. Sam was a victim of corporate downsizing and is spending his final working years in a position that is not satisfying. These difficult adjustments are made easier by the support of good friends and strong ties with extended family. But many couples at this stage do not experience the support of friends and family. These marriages are particularly vulnerable to divorce.

What can the parish do?

- Intergenerational parish programs offer social support and opportunities for faith reflection for couples who are alone. Some couples in the post-parenting years pull back from parish life after years of active leadership. Others spend their newly acquired free time and energy on opportunities for new growth and service in their parish. Parish leaders can tap into these couples' wisdom and experience if they establish a practice of teaching senior adults how to mentor those who will follow them in leadership.

- Anniversary celebrations that hold up long-term marriages before the community are one way of supporting married couples in this stage. Some parishes or dioceses hold annual marriage celebrations with renewal of vows and acknowledgment of longest married couples.

Other parishes honor special anniversaries at Sunday Mass or post on bulletin boards the pictures of couples married more than twenty-five years. This practice acknowledges that marriage is a sacramental sign for the whole community.

- Ongoing marriage enrichment opportunities at this stage can serve both couples and parish life. Excellent program materials are available and deal with the special concerns and strengths of post-childrearing couples. These materials help couples reflect on marital commitment, which is so necessary at this stage. Mature couples, who have more time to volunteer, also make excellent mentor couples who can assist in the parish or diocesan marriage preparation process. Couples who take part in this ministry say that it stimulates their own growth and development in faith.

The Later Years

What is going on?

Sam and Sandy join their retired friends at the Saturday evening Mass. They all go to an early dinner together afterward. This is a routine they started when Sam retired. Their concerns revolve around the widowed friends that have joined them for their Saturday night ritual, as well as their children and grandchildren who live in other cities far away.

Sam and Sandy are part of a population in the pews that is growing dramatically. Because of increased life expectancy and improved medical care, they are living longer and staying active well into their later years. Most have retired by their mid-60s and share similar concerns about adjustments in marriages where the focus of one spouse's life was work. More time together at home, a fixed income, and increasing health issues are all a part of the challenge of this stage.

Both of their parents are gone, and Sandy recently lost her older sister with whom she was very close. Sam and Sandy are in relatively good health, with the exception of Sam's failing eyesight. Though retirement has brought them many joys, such as a renewed appreciation and tolerance for one another and more opportunity to travel and enjoy life, they find themselves attending more funerals and making regular visits to friends who are ill. Like many of their peers, Sam and Sandy enjoy grandparenting from a distance, and they treasure the love and support of their children and grandchildren.

But many older adults are separated from family and have not kept up close intergenerational connections. They experience isolation and, when ill, must depend on others in their immediate community to assist them. Because women generally outlive men by seven years, there are many widows in this life stage who experience loneliness and the disadvantages of limited income. Though women are generally supportive of their peers who are widowed, men are more likely to live alone and tend to be more socially isolated unless they remarry.

There is enormous diversity among adults in the later years from sixty-five until death. Many are healthy and active. Others are physically limited and may be homebound and unable to drive while some are seriously infirm and are either living with family or in an institution.

While most adults enjoy the benefits that come from a life of work and investment in family, all adults in this stage face the spiritual challenge of adjusting to the limitations of age, and preparing for their own death or the death of their spouse. Their general well-being and happiness depend on health and financial issues, on their attitude toward aging, and upon the support they receive from family and community.

What can the parish do?

- Parishes can tap into the wisdom, experience, and available time that retired members of the community possess. When inviting them to take an active part in community, allow those who travel throughout the year and those who deal with physical limitations to adjust their commitments to parish accordingly. My sixty-seven-year-old brother and his wife lead a "Prime Timers" retirement group at their parish, and are relieved of their duties during the winter when they move to a warmer climate. This allows them to remain a vital part of parish life with ongoing opportunities for spiritual and social development.

- A consistent and well-organized outreach to grieving adults is an essential dimension of parish adult formation. The loss of loved ones can bring on a crisis of faith. A believing faith community can be the face of Christ to those in grief, whether it be a meal brought to the home, or a program that provides information on the grieving process, or a widow/widower support group. In some cases, reconciliation is needed after a death or serious loss. Trained grief ministers can provide leadership for parishes in offering opportunities for support and education at these difficult times. In the face of grief and loss, adult formation can take place in the practice of Christian charity for both those offering it and those receiving it.

- Some dioceses and groups of parishes provide annual conferences, retreats, and networks for aging adults. These events address later-life concerns such as marital adjustment to retirement, caring for ill or infirm spouses, physical fitness and health, financial planning, end-of-life issues and planning, living with Alzheimer's, grandparenting, and other matters of interest to older adults. The Christian community must address these issues because each is linked to personal faith belief and practice.

Crises That Impact Adult Development

Most challenges of adult growth along the life cycle are accompanied by joys and rewards that come from the new stage. But there are also crises that challenge adult growth and development that can, at the same time, be profound opportunities for psychological and spiritual transformation. Marital infidelity, bankruptcy, the death of a child, domestic or sexual abuse, and drug, sex, or alcohol addiction are some of the life crises that occur among people in the pews. When couples or individuals are hurting, they sometimes isolate themselves from parish life at the very time they are most in need. Grieving a profound loss, rebuilding, and moving on are critical dimensions of adult growth.

Parish faith formation leaders can presume that at any one time, dozens of parishioners are in these situations. In most cases such situations are not acknowledged or recognized as opportunities for adult faith growth. No households are exempt from such family crises, and a parish's ability to provide a unique like-to-like support and referral system for adults when they are hurting is an essential aspect of its mission.

Many peer support groups and ministries for couples in crisis exist on the diocesan and community level. Such groups assist couples in healing during their painful situation with a faith perspective. Programs such as Retrouvaille and The Third Option provide education, support, and spiritual formation for couples in crisis.

A parish that openly acknowledges the normalcy of such seasons of pain and loss and regularly informs its members about the availability of resources for families in crisis provides an open door for continuing adult formation over a lifetime. In large parishes where small, intimate faith sharing groups are established, couples often find the safety and acceptance among friends necessary during a crisis. In smaller communities where anonymity is so important, other methods of acknowledging the existence of such life crises can be used.

Notifying parish members about existing resources can be done with pamphlets in community spaces, written and oral referrals to community services, books and video resources in parish libraries, parish Web site information, and peer ministry contacts in parish directories. Some parishes provide pastoral counselors or therapists with sliding scale fees to see parishioners. Pastoral leaders who ignore or deny that Christian households experience such crises are overlooking an opportunity to provide adult formation at life's most vulnerable moments, and may be ignoring persons in their time of need.

Divorce, Single Again, and Remarriage in the Life Cycle

What is happening?
Ted and Theresa no longer come to Mass on Sunday together. Theresa arrives with the three children in tow and sits in back of church, hoping no one will notice she is there. She wants to avoid people's questions and comments about the divorce. She hopes to continue to participate in the faith community and wonders if her divorce status will exclude her from the activities she has enjoyed in the parish.

For Ted, the divorce has been a crisis of faith causing him to sever many of his previous connections. He has moved out of his home and into another parish. Going to church alone is difficult; he may give it one or two tries to see if he feels comfortable. If he finds a place where he fits in, he may stay; if not, he will see this part of his life as another failure.

Ted and Theresa experience feelings of anger, regret, helplessness, loss of control over their lives, and alienation from family and friends. Changes in relationships with immediate family, extended family, friends, work, school, and parish are a source of great stress for both of them. In addition to the normal developmental adult tasks of forty-seven-year-olds, they must learn to live alone again, to co-parent while separated, and to handle finances, social engagements, and extended family responsibilities as single-again persons. During their initial stage of divorce, they are more focused on how to manage day to day. If they come to their parish for support they will not want to feel judged as a failure.

The divorce process has its own developmental stages and tasks that overlay normal adult growth. Like the stages of grief, they can be occasions for profound spiritual transformation. Like any crisis that throws adults into chaos and disequilibrium, divorce is a spiritual crisis as well. In parishes where there is no support for or acknowledgment of the presence of divorced persons, the door to growth and healing is closed.

What can the parish do?

Research indicates that most adults need at least one to three years to engage in the divorce process before returning to stability and gaining a measure of control over their lives. A faith perspective is important in facing and working through the hurt and anger that accompany divorce.

Two pastoral strategies can be helpful here. The first is for pastoral leaders of all ministries to recognize that between one-third and one-half of Catholic marriages end in divorce. This impacts every area of parish life: adult formation, RCIA and other evangelization ministries, sacramental preparation programs, parish social and service organizations, and so on. Some parish leaders still find it difficult to openly acknowledge and welcome divorced persons into parish life, to accommodate programs to meet their needs, to place them in leadership when appropriate, and to acknowledge their presence openly in homilies, written communications, and parish planning. There remains some fear that full acceptance of divorced families will undermine the focus on marital fidelity. Until that fear is overcome, the church's ability to provide education and formation for divorcing Catholics will be severely limited.

The second strategy is for the parish to provide ongoing like-to-like ministry for its members who are separated, divorced, widowed, and remarried. Persons who have been through one of these experiences, and have grown through the stages of loss and rebuilding, can provide an effective support community for others in similar situations. Though it is never simple to create effective pastoral responses to persons who are in a process of loss and recovery, there are some effective, well established peer ministries that offer adult growth opportunities to assist divorced persons in negotiating this difficult transition.

- The North American Conference for Separated and Divorced Catholics (NACSDC) is a national organization with a variety of resources and training options for ministry to widowed, separated, and divorced persons. A national network of volunteers provides education, outreach, and support for parish leaders of divorce ministry and for divorcing persons. Other resources a parish might offer include the "Beginning Experience" Weekend, coping sessions for widowed, separated, and divorced, and "Rainbows for All God's Children" with its accompanying parent programs. These and many more such resources provide adult formation during a period of traumatic life transition. Parish leadership can make referrals to such programs if they are not available locally.

- Offer annulment information sessions. Because five-sixths of men and three-fourths of women who divorce will eventually re-marry, it is essential to provide opportunities for healing and continued personal faith growth for divorcing persons. Many divorced persons leave the church because of confusion and frustration over the annulment process. Pastoral care and education for divorced persons are essential if they are to remain active and open to growth in faith. Since so much misinformation exists about divorce and remarriage, parish staff should be familiar with basic information and referrals for the annulment process. Many parishes have informative pamphlets and offer an annual information program on the annulment process.
- Create stepfamily and blended family education and support groups. Parish marriage preparation and baptismal preparation programs are welcoming more second-married and blended families every year. These adults experience additional challenges at home because they are often facing double developmental tasks at once. They may be adjusting to a new spouse, or having a baby while caring for aging parents. If both have brought children into the marriage, the challenges increase. In these situations, peer ministry is an effective way to help adults in their struggle to continue growing when they are feeling overwhelmed. Such marriages are at greater risk of divorce than first-time marriages, so enrichment and support are important particularly in the first years of adjustment.

Cultural Diversity and Life Cycle Development

What is happening?

A sea of new faces is filling Catholic churches. Baptisms, weddings, and confirmations reflect the color, dress, social patterns, and traditions of immigrant and minority Catholics in the American church. In addition to the more familiar Black and Native American ethnic groups are the European, Hispanic, and Asian ethnic groupings, each of which includes diverse sub-groups. These groups both enrich and challenge parish life and adult formation efforts.

Though there are many commonalities in the way adults mature along the life cycle, a rich diversity exists within that unity. What it means to be a faithful husband or wife in a Hispanic or Asian family may involve different tasks and skills than in an Anglo household. The role of children, parents, grandparents, and godparents differs among cultures. An immigrant family from the Sudan will have different expectations, rituals, and coping mechanisms at any point in the life cycle than will most middle-class Americans. Awareness of such diverse patterns of growth is essential to a parish's design and execution of adult formation programs.

What can the parish do?

Parishes and diocesan offices all over the United States are responding to their growing immigrant and minority populations. One West Coast diocese offers marriage preparation classes in thirty-seven languages. Baptismal programs and other sacramental preparation aids continue to be translated and culturally adapted. More textbooks, liturgical aids, and Catholic resources are produced in Spanish to meet the needs of a burgeoning Catholic Hispanic population.

Hiring ethnic minorities in parish positions is helpful, but if that is not possible, an effective and realistic alternative exists. Numerous diocesan and parish programs of adult formation across the country have trained more established immigrant leaders to advocate for the special needs of recently arrived populations. In Omaha, local Latino leaders provide a series of five Sunday afternoon education and formation classes for couples who were married civilly in Mexico or elsewhere and who wish to have their marriages blessed in the church. This need surfaced because Spanish-speaking baptismal preparation leaders discovered that parents bringing their babies for baptism were not sacramentally married in the church. For those who are not bilingual, first-language resources and speakers are essential.

The work of providing adult formation opportunities that are sensitive to the growing number of diverse ethnic populations is a complex and long-term project. At a recent training for baptismal preparation facilitators, I encountered an African immigrant who was struggling, not with the language of the program, but with the assumption in the baptismal materials of the equality of husband and wife and the stance that both mother and father share responsibility for the care of the baby when both are at home. She told me emphatically that this notion would not be accepted by her people who held radically different views on gender roles in marriage. To be able to offer adult formation at the time of baptism, the program's content on family as domestic church had to be adapted for these families. That adaptation had to be done by representatives of that ethnic minority and the authors of the material.

Such changes will be required for many years to come so that integration into Catholic parish life both brings about Christian unity and respects the uniqueness of each culture represented in it. The church has nothing to lose in this effort, but a rich multicultural treasure to gain, making a Catholic church even more catholic in word and deed.

Conclusion

In *Our Hearts Were Burning within Us*, the U.S. bishops remind us that "to be effective ministers of adult faith formation we will first, like Jesus, join people in their daily concerns and walk side by side with them on the pathways of life. We will ask them questions and listen attentively as they speak of their joys, hopes, griefs, and anxieties" (pp. 2-3). In order to do this effectively, it is important for pastoral leaders to know as much as possible about the joys, hopes, griefs, and anxieties of adult growth. Understanding the growth process taking place in married couples within the domestic church can assist leaders in bringing the gospel and the support of Christian community to adult Catholics across the life cycle.

Reflection Questions

1. How do you think the faith formation currently offered at your parish makes connections between faith and everyday life for couples at various stages of marriage?
2. Do you think separated, divorced, or widowed persons feel welcome or included in your parish? Why or why not?
3. Some leaders find it difficult to promote the dignity of marriage while also including and ministering to those whose marriages have ended. How do you deal with that tension? What practical ministry advice would you offer to a parish wrestling with that tension?

References

United States Conference of Catholic Bishops. *Our Hearts Were Burning within Us*. Washington, DC: USCCB Publishing, 1999.

Chapter Four

Connecting Life & Faith

Leif Kehrwald
(See bio on page 26)

EDITOR'S NOTE

The first three chapters of this book have attempted to articulate some of both the ideals and the realities of family life. Chapter 1 presents a beautiful argument for the holy and sacred nature of family life. By definition it is idealistic; but that does not render the argument any less valid. Chapters 2 and 3 describe the developmental realities facing families and couples. We are now ready to bring the ideals and realities together. This chapter addresses the foundational concepts for helping families connect daily life with faith practice. The following chapter offers four concrete steps to help families do just that.

Some parents and families approach faith practice as just one of many, many "shoulds" in their busy lives. They know they should worship on Sunday and participate in other parish activities, but they are bombarded from every direction with expectations about how to spend their limited time. In response to parish expectations, more than one parent has muttered, "You have no idea what it's like for us in our family."

Actually, we parish leaders—those of us who work with families in the context of our ministries—do have some idea. We may not know the particular stressors in any one family's home, but the realities of family and household life are all too apparent.

Time. Too much to do, too many places to be, not enough hours in the day to accomplish it all.

Energy. Raising a family is an high-energy endeavor. One quickly learns to take shortcuts to preserve energy wherever and whenever possible.

Relationships. While nurturing, rewarding, and essentially the source of all life, relationships are also complicated, confusing, and troubling at times.

Money. For most, there simply is not enough. For nearly all, finances create stress that lingers and is ever present.

Media and Pop-culture. The consumeristic, instant-gratification, highly-sexed values of the contemporary culture create an "us vs. the world" mentality that sucks every ounce of energy out of us and often feels like a losing battle.

As parish leaders, you and I know these realities. You see them every-day. You, of course, could easily add to the list. Yet these same realities are present among those who have somehow figured out how to make faith and religious practice part of the picture of their family life. How do they do that? Where do they find the time, energy, focus, and desire to make faith and religious practice a priority in their complicated lives?

This chapter seeks to respond to certainly one of the most common questions among parish ministers who work with families: How do we help families recognize that the ordinary (and extraordinary) experiences of their daily lives are connected to God and the Catholic faith?

Breakfast on the Beach

From a theological and scriptural perspective, let's turn our attention to John's gospel and the story of breakfast on the beach (John 21). Peter, James, John, and the others announce they are going fishing. Jesus had just died, and they didn't know what else to do. It's late in the day; they fish all night and catch nothing.

At first light, a man on the shore calls out to them, imploring them to toss their nets on the other side of the boat. They are bewildered because no one ever fishes over that side of the boat. But realizing their hold is empty, they think: what have we to lose? They toss their nets on the other side and they catch such a large load of fish they cannot haul it aboard.

John looks to the man on the shore and declares it is the Lord! Peter gets so excited he puts his clothes on and jumps in the water to swim to shore. Meanwhile, the others haul the fish in.

When they arrive, the man beckons them to gather around the fire to break bread and share fish. As they share the meal, we're told, none has to ask who the man is, for they know it is the Lord.

What followed was an extraordinary exchange between Jesus and Peter; in truth, this was an extraordinary reconciliation.

Jesus said to Simon Peter, "Simon son of John, do you love me more than these?" He said to him, "Yes, Lord; you know that I love you." Jesus said to him, "Feed my lambs." A second time he said to him, "Simon son of John, do you love me?" He said to him, "Yes, Lord; you know that I love you." Jesus said to him, "Tend my sheep." He said to him the third time, "Simon son of John, do you love me?" Peter felt hurt because he said to him the third time, "Do you love me?" And he said to him, "Lord, you know everything; you know that I love you." Jesus said to him, "Feed my sheep." (John 21:15–17)

In this exchange, Jesus gives Peter the opportunity to declare his love, right out loud, in front of all the others, to repent of his three adamant denials just a few days earlier.

"Breakfast on the beach" is a story of family life and faith experience. The family—Jesus and his friends who had become quite familial over the previous three years or so—was challenged to grow and change, stay in touch with their roots, and reconcile a serious rift. As families negotiate the challenges of transition and change, they are constantly forced to "toss their nets on the other side," conduct themselves in new ways, with each new development and new stage.

But families must also stay rooted to the practices and activities that bring them together and reinforce their love for each other in order to effectively heal their hurts and difficulties. The reconciliation between Jesus and Peter is predicated on the meal just shared by all. When families spend time together, share meals, hang out with each other in un-programmed time, they empower themselves to reconcile their conflicts.

Moments of Meaning

Every day, families experience what I call "moments of meaning" that have the potential to become religiously significant. Aside from those extraordinary moments when God's grace explodes in the face of the family, many ordinary moments may go by undetected, let alone reflected upon. To probe their religious significance, someone in the family must point it out, and then the family must acknowledge it and respond to it. (Chapter Five outlines a four-step process the family can learn in order to mine the religious significance of the moment of meaning.)

In his classic book *An Experience Named Spirit*, John Shea writes,

…there are moments which, although they occur within the everyday confines of human living, take on larger meaning. They have a lasting impact; they cut through to something deeper; they demand a hearing. It may be the death of a parent, the touch of a friend, falling in love, a betrayal, the recognition of what has really been happening over the last two years, the unexpected arrival of blessing, the sudden advent of curse. But whatever it is, we sense we have undergone something that has touched upon the normally dormant but always present relationship to God. (p. 97)

As parish ministers we seek to help families recognize God's gracious presence in their daily lives, and we show them how the Christian tradition can illuminate their experience, turning "ordinary" human moments into religiously significant moments. We can help families develop the skill to make connections between experience and faith, not in the way we do it in formal learning programs, but in the ordinary way Jesus connected life to the sacred: through stories and symbols, gestures and embraces, questions and conversations.

Many Types of Moments

The moments of meaning that occur in family life are infinite. They all have potential for spiritual growth and faith formation. Yet, in my experience, attempts to immediately put faith-based language and labels on these moments sometimes shrouds their powerful meaning. In other words, if we attempt to interpret all life experience through the same lens, then life itself becomes benign and pedestrian, no matter what the lens.

Yet some categorization can help make sense of the moment. Think of it this way: families have spiritual encounters when engaged in religious and faith-based activities. That's one good category. But we also know that families have spiritual encounters when engaged in a whole host of other activities that are not overtly religious or faith-based. These encounters may fall into one or more of the following categories: food and meals, conversation, media, education, trauma and trouble, service to others, worship and gathering, angst over decision-making, work and labor, illness and health care, travel, leisure and rest, and certainly a host of additional categories. God is present in these encounters just as God is present in organized religious activities.

Some of these encounters can be predicted and anticipated, such as a birthday, holiday, anniversary, and so on. The family may choose to bring forth the spiritual connection in any of these moments by composing a prayer, or conducting a simple blessing, or talking about these occassions from a faith perspective. More often, the parent or family *would like* to acknowledge the spirituality of these moments, but just doesn't know how to do so.

Other encounters arrive unannounced and unanticipated. The spiritually "nimble" family may inherently recognize the power of the moment, and proceed to break open its spiritual meaning and benefit. But, as you know, most families in their busy-ness and rushed lives will fail to recognize God's presence, and will simply seek to process it as quickly as possible, or give it no heed whatsoever, and move on.

The Jesus Story

We seek to help families filter their experiences through the lens of faith and spirituality—no small task—and develop a faith rapport with one another. This is, among other things, a faith formation issue. We seek to help families connect their stories with the stories of Jesus. Becoming familiar with the stories of Jesus, therefore, becomes paramount. Yet, we must think of faith formation in the broadest possible terms, recognizing that all of us are formed in faith through a wide variety of media, of which formal religious education plays only a part. Regardless of the medium, the formation is always personal and usually rather intimate. Shea puts it this way:

> It is people, always people who are handing on the memory of Jesus. We have access to the Jesus story through a chain of mediation, a long line of personal appropriation and retellings. It is through a parent's instructive voice or the evangelist's artful writing or a Zeffirelli's camera that the story is made available. This does not deny the normative nature of the gospel rendition or the need for a teaching authority to correctly interpret it. It merely underlines the personal nature of community and tradition. (*An Experience Named Spirit*, p. 114)

We seek to help families become intentional about their faith growth by connecting their informal faith experiences with the formal religious practice of the community. Sounds simple enough, right? Most Catholic families want faith to be a meaningful part of their lives, so with a little nudge, some instructional encouragement, and a few helpful resources they should take right off, shouldn't they? As your own ministerial experience tells you, not necessarily. Seemingly, only the "best" Catholic families respond to such assistance, and they would likely pursue their family spirituality even if your assistance were not available.

Why the lackluster response? I submit that over the last several generations the institutional church has conditioned a more or less passive response to family faith formation rather than an intentional response. We have conditioned families, particularly parents, into a rather narrow job description in the grand scheme of faith formation: deliver your children and teens to all parish programs, and bring them to Mass on Sunday.

Without stating it overtly, we have communicated a message to parents and families that can be blithely summed up like this: "Give us your children and teens in September, and we will give you disciples in May." Of course, this statement is myth, but the institutional church has convinced many parents that the only faith formation worth its salt occurs in the parish education center. To top it off, we toss in a little confusion by continually reminding parents that they are the "primary educators of their children." It's no wonder we encounter many parents in our programs who, while they would never use these words, seem to say to us, "Here are my children and teens. Just do unto them what you did unto me a generation ago. I'll pick them up upon my return from Wal-Mart."

When we help families get in touch with the moments of meaning in their lives, and we model simple steps they can take to garner the religious significance of those moments, then they will become more intentional about their informal faith practice at home *and* their participation in the formal religious practice of the community. When we model for families ways to reflect upon experience and talk with each other about it, they become empowered to engage in similar practice at home.

Parishes engaged in intergenerational learning are discovering a valuable format for modeling this kind of faith formation. When all generations are brought together for learning, the only things that bridge developmental differences among the age groups are stories and experiences. A good story cuts across all developmental lines and allows the listener to hear the meaning and message that are appropriate for them. Intergenerational settings are ideal for putting family stories in dialogue with the Jesus story. "Putting together our story with the story of Jesus is the way we discover the movement of the divine in our lives....Only if we have found God in the Jesus story will we use that story to talk about the God of our own story" (*An Experience Named Spirit*, p. 112).

In summary, as is mentioned above, we seek to *help families recognize that the ordinary (and extraordinary) experiences of their daily lives are connected to God and the Catholic faith.* In order to do this, we must help families

- become aware of the moments of meaning in their lives,
- filter their experiences through the lens of faith and spirituality,
- become aware of God's gracious presence in their lives and respond to it,
- develop a faith rapport with one another,

- connect their informal faith experiences with the formal religious practice of the community,
- become intentional about their desire to grow in faith.

A tall order, you may think. Indeed, it is! Yet, we must keep two things in mind.

First, some families are doing these things already. Some families have found creative and meaningful ways to connect their life experiences with faith growth. They *are* intentional about it, and it is much more than just another "should" in their busy lives.

Second, as parish leaders, we don't have a choice but to move in this direction. We all know that the existing school-house model of faith education—all by itself—is bankrupt and simply does not work. Perhaps there was a time, several generations ago, when Catholic faith and practice were deeply enculturated in families and neighborhoods, allowing the CCD model to actually work. The content of the classroom had a foundational context in which to grow within the enculturated Catholic home. Those days are over. Our task of faith formation is much more complex and comprehensive now, and we must not be afraid to employ new models and new methodologies to account for that complexity. The simple structure of the classroom as the only instructional tool will not suffice.

Seven Key Principles

As a starting point, if we want parents and families to be intentional about their faith growth, then the parish leader must become much more intentional and strategic about empowering them to do so.

The Christian tradition has always recognized that God is active in the ordinary and extraordinary events in our lives. God lingers in the creases and folds of family living. When the family becomes aware of God's gracious activity in their lives, they are challenged to respond, both for the sake of their own faith growth and for the sake of the larger community. Parish leaders are challenged to assist them.

Pope John Paul II recognized the variety of ways that families grow in faith. In *Familiaris Consortio* he outlined four distinct, but interdependent tasks for families: form a loving community, serve life by bearing and educating children, participate in building a caring and just society, share in the life and mission of the church.

The *General Directory for Catechesis* reinforces Pope John Paul II's challenges to families when it states:

The family is defined as a "domestic church," that is, in every Christian family the different aspects and functions of the life of the entire church may be reflected: mission; catechesis; witness; prayer etc. Indeed in the same way as the Church, the family "is a place in which the Gospel is transmitted and from which it extends." The family as a *locus* of catechesis has an unique privilege: transmitting the Gospel by rooting it in the context of profound human values....It is, indeed, a Christian education more witnessed to than taught, more occasional than systematic, more ongoing and daily than structured into periods. (#255)

The U.S. bishops also understood this dynamic when they wrote their pastoral message to families, *Follow the Way of Love*, and outlined four particular challenges to families: live faithfully, give life, grow in mutuality, take time together.

And the new *National Directory for Catechesis* reinforces the U.S. bishops' vision in this statement:

The Christian family is ordinarily the first experience of the Christian community and the primary environment for growth in faith. Because it is the "church of the home" (FC 38), the family provides a unique *locus* for catechesis. It is a place in which the word of God is received and from which it is extended. With the Christian family, parents are the primary educators in the faith and "the first heralds of the faith with regard to their children" (LG 11). But all the members make up the family, and each can make a unique contribution to creating the basic environment in which a sense of God's loving presence is awakened and faith in Jesus Christ is confessed, encouraged, and lived. (p. 100-101)

It can also be said that the traditional Christian expressions of ministry understand that families come to faith and grow through a variety of responses. Let me reacquaint you with these Greek expressions:

Didache—sharing the Catholic faith story.

Koinonia—relating to the wider community.

Kerygma—enriching one another with the Word of God.

Diakonia—responding to those in need.

Leiturgia—celebrating rituals and praying together.

The point here is to help us see that there are a variety of channels through which God's initiative touches family life and then, in turn, the family responds and grows in faith. It's not enough to simply declare that the Christian family is holy and sacred, and, therefore, all the events in the life of that family are potential moments of faith growth. While this is certainly true, the vastness of possibilities may render both the family and the parish leader blind to all but the most obvious. Therefore, categorizing these experiences allows for practical application of resources, assistance, and connection with others in the community who may have had similar encounters.

The following principles form a framework for your strategic response in helping families make the connection. These principles recognize the full range of faith encounters that families can have, yet offer seven separate categories from which to offer pastoral assistance and effective resources. These principles can also give guidance for one's efforts to conduct all parish programs and services in a family-friendly manner.

Also, notice the repeated connection between faith and ordinary life. Imagine helping the family place their moment of meaning into one of these responses, and assisting their learning in that context.

1. *Intentional.* Parents are the first and most influential educators of their children. Families provide the foundational setting in which a young person's faith is formed. Does the moment of meaning connect to the parents' role as primary faith educators?

2. *Daily Life.* Families grow in faith when they "stop, look, and listen" in order to recognize God's gracious activity in their daily lives. Does the moment of meaning connect to the ordinary or extraordinary events of daily life?

3. *Wholeness and Well-being.* When families build healthy relationships with each other through positive interactions, sharing meals, solving conflicts, and the like, they also grow in faith together. Does the moment of meaning connect to maintaining, healing, or enriching family relationships?

4. *Change.* While sometimes resisted, moments of change and transition in family life open windows for faith growth. Several predictable transitions correspond with sacramental moments. Does the moment of meaning connect to an experience of change or transition in the family?

5. *Religious Practice.* When families practice their faith—through conversation and discussion, ritual and celebration, outreach and service to others—they grow in faith together. Does the moment of meaning connect to religious activity in the home or in the larger faith community?

6. *Worship.* When families participate in the liturgical feasts, seasons, and rhythms of the church, they make connections between their faith encounters and the faith life of the larger community. Does the

moment of meaning connect to the worship celebrations of the faith community?

7. *Contemporary Culture.* Families meet the challenges of contemporary culture by articulating their values, establishing clear priorities, and making careful decisions—all in an atmosphere of community support. Does the moment of meaning connect to the family's relationship with society and popular culture?

When family members, particularly adults and teens in the family, are familiar with and understand these seven principles, two things occur quite readily. First, they will recognize the moments of meaning that occur in their families more easily and more often. Second, they will have a clearer sense of how to respond to the movement of the Spirit in a way that benefits all.

The next chapter outlines a four-step process families can take to connect their moments of meaning to a life of faith. These are teachable steps that can be modeled for families by bringing them together, demonstrating the steps, coaching and nurturing them, and providing them with helpful resources along the way.

Reflection Questions

1. Do you agree with the following statement? Why or why not?

   Without stating it overtly, we have communicated a message to parents and families that can be blithely summed up like this: "Give us your children and teens in September, and we will give you disciples in May." Of course, this statement is myth, but the institutional church has convinced many parents that the only faith formation worth its salt occurs in the parish education center.

2. What can we do to help families take a more active faith formation role with each other in their homes?

3. What do you think of the seven principles for family faith formation? Would you add to the list? If yes, what? How could these principles be used to help families grow in faith?

References

Congregation for the Clergy. *General Directory for Catechesis.* Washington, DC: United States Catholic Conference, 1998.

Shea, John. *An Experience Named Spirit.* Allen, TX: Thomas More, 1983.

United State Conference of Catholic Bishops. *National Directory for Catechesis.* Washington, DC: USCCB Publishing, 2005.

Chapter Five

Practical Steps for Connecting Life & Faith

Leif Kehrwald

(See bio on page 26)

Editor's Note

This chapter offers a simple four-step process designed to help families notice their moments of meaning, reflect upon them, put them in dialogue with the Jesus story, and see what difference it can make in their lives. I have worked with numerous groups of parents and families. Given a conducive atmosphere, I can attest that the four steps work. When parents and families are given the opportunity to work through the four steps, they actually do begin to connect their daily life with their faith practice.

The following four-step process can be modeled and taught to families to help them connect the realities of their lives with their faith, and consequently become more immersed in the life of the faith community. The steps are outlined sequentially only for the sake of clarity. A parish director of religious education recently commented that perhaps they should just be called "elements" for connecting life and faith, eliminating any indication of sequence. Yet, while no family, no individual, will follow these steps to a T, there seems to be a natural progression from one to the next. And these steps are teachable. When learned, families will begin to discover that they are indeed making the connection between the craziness of their lives and the presence of God in their midst.

The process helps families pause and take a look at what's happening—become present to the moment—and then purposefully engage in several sequenced steps that lead them toward a spiritually-based interpretation of what's happening. The key, of course, is intention. These steps will help the family mine the sacredness of the key moments of their lives.

What do I mean by "moment"? It means just what you think it means: an event, encounter, or circumstance that presents itself to the family in the present time. We want to help the family become aware of *now*. A baby takes her first steps. A teen gets his driver's license. An argument is resolved and siblings reconcile. These are but a few of the infinite possibilities for encounter.

But "moment" can also mean the state of circumstance into which the family has fallen without any corporate awareness of having done so. As an example, consider a family with adolescent children who is so caught up in the busy-ness of their lives—school, work, after-school activities, church, and so on—that they unwittingly slip into a pattern of functioning without talking to each other beyond the minimum of surface conversation. When one or two family members become aware of their circumstance, they can begin the change process.

Four-Step Process

A "moment of meaning" has just occurred. For the family to fully benefit from what the moment has to teach, I suggest that they need to engage in four distinct steps:

1. *Awareness. Stop! Look! Listen!*

   Someone recognizes that the family is having a moment of meaning. Someone points it out to everyone else so that all are aware.

2. *Acknowledge It!*

   As a whole, the family acknowledges the presence of the Spirit in their midst. The routine of ordinary life is disrupted to make room to embrace the new experience.

3. *Connect to the Sacred.*

   The family either chooses to pursue this process further, or to let it go. Questions to consider:

   - How does our story connect to the Jesus story?
   - How do we pray about this encounter, or, how does this encounter change our prayer?
   - Who are the wisdom people with whom we should connect?
   - How does this encounter intersect with the life of our faith community and our religious practice?

4. *So What?*

> What difference has this experience made in our lives? What memory have we created? How will we revisit it? What have we learned? How will it change our behavior?

These steps are easily taught by parish leaders and learned pretty easily by families. Let's take a closer look at each step through the lens of several vignettes of family moments of meaning. We will use the stories of "Spring Musical," "Christmas Homecoming," "Oregon Coast," and "Taco Salad" to deepen our understanding of each step. The beginning of each family vignette is included below, and an additional piece to each story is added under the description of each step later in this chapter.

Unanticipated Moment: Spring Musical

Josh is a high school senior who loves music, dance, and drama. Throughout his high school career he has landed only minor parts in the school drama productions. He had always felt that his true talent had not been fully recognized until one January afternoon, he arrived home and announced, "I got the lead in the Spring musical!"

Rite of Passage: Christmas Homecoming

Last Spring Melissa graduated from high school, and then in the Fall she went off to college. Like many her age, it was her first experience of being away from home for an extended time. Since her school is across the country from her family, she has not seen them until now, during Christmas vacation.

After being away for nearly four months, Melissa relishes the familiar surroundings of home, but she also realizes that nearly everything has changed. For one thing, it surprises her that she missed her family and her home; just a few months earlier she couldn't wait to get away from them. Yet her parents, even her younger siblings, have been really fun to hang out with. They are interested in her new life, and—here's the surprising part—Melissa is interested in them!

Melissa can't remember when their family holiday traditions have been so meaningful for her as they are this year. And she keeps having these lovely, nostalgic memories of her early childhood—triggered by simple things such as smells, smiles, a song on the radio, a TV commercial. Melissa is observing herself with her family, and she likes what she sees.

Annual Moment: Oregon Coast

It was nearing the end of Summer, and our boys (then in grade school) were bored and disillusioned. While they hadn't said as much, they both had hoped for something fun and exciting before school started. My wife and I had too much work to do, so it just wasn't possible...or, so they thought.

One afternoon, we told them we had to run across town to the mall.

"Do we have to go?" they asked.

"Of course! We're not going to leave you home alone," we responded.

"Why not go to the mall near our house?"

"They don't have the store at our mall so we have to go across town. Come on, get in the car."

We loaded into the car and hit the freeway. Each son immediately zoned out into his own world in the backseat. I just kept driving. It's a thirty-minute drive to the mall across town.

An hour went by and the car was quiet. It finally donned on our oldest that we hadn't arrived at the mall. "Hey, what's going on?" he asked.

"Don't worry, we'll be there soon," answered Rene in her effort to placate them a little while longer.

No such luck, of course. Suddenly they knew something was up, and they demanded an explanation. Our getaway had been clean and flawless, so we took great pleasure in springing our surprise of a two-night Bed and Breakfast stay on the Oregon Coast. Their eyes lit up with delight, and we knew then that we had already created a lasting family memory.

I don't remember much about that trip, other than how happy we were to be together and to get away from home. Rene and I often recall the joy we shared in planning for that excursion, packing up clothes for the boys and sneaking them into the car, enjoying their oblivion as we sailed past the mall on our way to the ocean. And the boys will never let us forget that trick we played on them. Someone will often mention it whenever we talk about good times together.

Delayed Reflection: Taco Salad

I anticipated an ordinary Summer evening: a simple dinner, taking an evening walk, perhaps paying some bills, catch a little TV, off to bed on the early side. Nothing special. It's not that I didn't want to be with my wife and sons, I just didn't want or need much of anything at all. Yet there were deeper, stronger forces afoot.

I popped into the kitchen to get a clue about dinner. Luke, then twelve years old, was the only one there.

"Luke, where's Mom?"

"She's upstairs," Luke responded. "Dad, where's the olive oil?"

"In the corner cupboard. Why?"

"I'm making dinner tonight!" he said with a sly smile. "We're having taco salad, and I need to make the dressing."

Knowing I was responsible for cleanup, and knowing Luke, I could visualize what the kitchen would look like once he finished preparing dinner. So I uncharacteristically said, "Luke, do you want some help?"

"Nope. Dad, I'm going to do this all by myself." His smile turned to a grin of determination.

What could I do, but begin right then to prepare myself for a long night of cleanup?

An hour later Luke called us all to the table and we feasted on a terrific taco salad. He was filled with pride as he told us every detail of making such a complicated meal. "It's best to use the large cheese grater rather than the small one....You have to stir the re-fried beans often or they'll stick to the pan....I had to wash the lettuce three times...," and on and on. He was so proud!

And we felt proud of him, too. The task of making taco salad is not so difficult, but on this one night our son really felt a genuine desire to be of service to his family. It was pure heart that motivated him, or perhaps pure grace.

Step One: Awareness: Stop! Look! Listen!

The first and most crucial step is for someone in the family to realize, "We're having a moment of meaning." Little alarm bells go off in that person's head. The event may be relatively benign, such as a resolution to a conflict, or a piece of good news, or an unexpected deed that someone performs simply out of the goodness of his or her heart. Or, it may be an extraordinary moment, such as a teenager's first love lost, or a child's first day of middle school, or the death of a loved one.

Instead of just enveloping this event into the routine of the day, someone must take notice that something important just happened, and then point it out to other family members. He or she must speak up and say, "Stop! Look what's happening here! Can we listen to what the Spirit wants to say to us at this very moment?"

It's a risk of vulnerability to bring it up and talk about it, especially when the person is not at all sure what it means or how to explain it. It's a gut feeling more than anything.

It's also a risk, because when a family member challenges the others to stop, look, and listen, then there had better be something to get excited about. Or it's risky because the others may not want to go there; their intuition tells them it may not be easy. They may be expected to be intimate with each other. They may have to reconcile with each other. They may be expected to do any number of things that bring them out of their protective shell and make them vulnerable with each other. It's easy to dismiss the gut feeling and let the moment of meaning pass.

Spring Musical

Growing up, Josh's mother dreamed of being a professional ballerina. Her dream never came true. When Josh announced his good news amid the noise and chaos of preparations for supper, Mom knew what a triumph this was for him. And she knew that unless she did something, the rest of the family would just let it go with a "That's great, Josh."

Christmas Homecoming

Melissa and her dad had lunch together downtown. She told him how strange it is that everything seems the same, and yet also completely different. "I guess I didn't know what a great family I have. I took you all for granted," Melissa told her dad. He responded, "We missed you a lot more than we had imagined. You were so ready to leave in August. It was difficult around the house, so we were a bit surprised at how deeply we felt your absence." Then, through their lunch date, they described how each family member has adapted and changed as a result of Melissa's launch into young adulthood. The lunch concludes with her dad telling Melissa that her younger sister would like to trade bedrooms.

"Oh, really?" was Melissa's response.

Oregon Coast

The intent all along was to create a family memory through this surprise. As mentioned, we enjoyed the planning as much as our boys enjoyed the surprise itself. This was an intentionally designed moment of meaning.

Taco Salad

The awareness of the moment of meaning came to me only in memory, and it has remained a personal "pearl of great price" that I carry in my heart. The memory endears my son to me, even though he is now a young adult with accomplished culinary skills.

Step Two: Acknowledge It!

In their own way, the family acknowledges that things are not the same as they were before the moment. Their routine of ordinary life has been disrupted so they can embrace this new encounter. They begin to recognize the presence of the Spirit in their midst.

This step also requires some intention, even leadership, by one or two people in the family. Even if they do not yet understand the full meaning of what is going on, they must trust intuition that is urging the whole family to venture into the encounter. As a whole, the family must be willing to allow the disruption. They must be willing to trust enough to go along this unexpected path to see what can happen.

Spring Musical

Mom gives Josh a congratulatory hug and announces to all, "Dinner will be ready in twenty minutes. Don't be late because we have something wonderful to celebrate!" When they all sit down for supper, Josh finds that he's been given the "special plate" reserved for special occasions and accomplishments. Everyone finds a wine glass at his or her place. Wine or juice is poured into the glasses, and Mom begins the meal with a toast to Josh. "It's not every day that one of our lifelong dreams comes true, but today, for Josh, one did. Hurray for Josh in landing the lead role in the Spring Musical!" Applause all around. The meal conversation centers on what the audition was like, how Josh selected and prepared his monologue and solo, and whether the director is aware that Josh, while a great actor and a good singer, is not a strong dancer. Later, the discussion flows into rehearsal schedules, performance dates, and arrangements for Grandma and Grandpa to come see the show.

Christmas Homecoming

A couple of evenings later, Melissa's younger sister brought up the bedroom issue. When her dad had mentioned this at lunch, Melissa was reluctant, even a little upset. But after thinking about it for a couple of days, she understood the practicality of the move. Her bedroom was bigger and it wasn't being used. The other family members had been braced for argument, but when Melissa didn't resist, they had a pleasant discussion about the benefits of each room, and they made plans for doing the swap.

Oregon Coast

When the surprise was sprung, everyone became aware of the powerful moment. Life as we knew it was completely disrupted in a powerfully good way. We felt close to each other, and we knew we could talk on a deeper level.

Taco Salad

I did not bring this experience to the whole family, because the opportunity had passed once I realized it was a moment of meaning. Yet it interrupted my life enough for me to recall it and write about it.

Step Three: Connect to the Sacred.

The individual and the family are now confronted with a basic choice: do they pursue this moment of meaning to see what it may teach, or do they let it go? Letting it go is a legitimate choice. The family may be in the midst of something else that needs their full energy and attention. For example, add to the "Taco Salad" story the factor that a family member is seriously ill or injured, and Luke made supper in order to relieve anxiety around the house. He would be thanked for his effort, and then everyone could turn their attention back to the major issue at hand.

Or, perhaps the moment of meaning touches on issues that family members simply have no desire to pursue at this time. Perhaps it will open wounds or areas of such vulnerability and sensitivity that they simply cannot deal with at this time.

If the family chooses not to pursue it, members owe some affirmation, support, and perhaps explanation to the one who recognized the moment and brought it to the family in the first place. That individual took all the right steps toward healthy faith growth. That person took a risk to bring it forward, and he or she should not be made to feel that the risk was not worth it. Whether child, teen, or adult, the person should be showered with support and encouragement.

If the family chooses to pursue the moment of meaning, they sense it can teach them something, and they are convinced it has implications for their spiritual well-being as a family. They want to mine its riches. How do they do so?

They have already cleared the most difficult hurdle: intention. They are intentional rather than passive about their growth around this experience. They are responsive rather than reactive.

With this intentional action, the family will seek answers to these five basic questions to help them reflect on the moment of meaning, and to glean what it has to teach them.

1. How does our story connect to the Jesus story?
2. How do we pray about this encounter, or how does this encounter change our prayer?
3. Who are the wisdom people with whom we should connect?
4. How does this encounter intersect with the life of our faith community and our religious practice?
5. What resources should we pursue for further growth?

When the family pursues answers these questions they will glean the learning and growth that the moment of meaning held for them. Let's briefly examine each question.

1. *How does our story connect to the Jesus story?*

   Is there a gospel story that connects to the encounter? What is the meaning and message behind that story? Does that message also apply to the encounter? What does the Bible say about this situation? What would Jesus do in this situation?

   As parish leaders, the challenge here is helping families become conversant in the Jesus story, the gospel stories that tell about the life, death, and resurrection of Jesus. We must take every possible opportunity to immerse them in the stories and encounters of Jesus.

2. *How do we pray about this encounter, or how does this encounter change our prayer?*

   Does the moment call for rejoicing or repentance? Does the encounter draw the family into intimate embrace and prayers of gratitude, or does it call for prayers for courage and resolve? Does it challenge the family to stand up for others, or call them to circle their wagons and draw in on themselves? What are the prayers, and what are the ways to pray in each of these circumstances?

   As parish leaders, we must help families broaden the ways they pray in order to accommodate the many different encounters. We must give them prayer tools, resources, and examples so that when their moments of meaning occur, they feel more empowered to find the best way to pray at that moment.

3. *Who are the wisdom people with whom we should connect?*

   Does the encounter require interpretation? To whom does the family turn for help in understanding it? Or does the event simply cry out to be shared with others in joy and happiness? Does the family have an outlet to do just that? Or does the moment of meaning call for comfort, support, and encouragement? To whom can the family turn? Or does the moment simply call for mutual commiseration from someone who's "been there"?

As parish leaders, we must help families build networks and connections with others who can supply the wisdom they seek. Often, like-to-like connections (peer ministry) are most effective. Getting people connected is one thing, but we must also create the conducive atmosphere so families feel safe sharing with one another. Intergenerational gatherings and faith formation sessions often create such an atmosphere.

4. *How does this encounter intersect with the life of our faith community and our religious practice?*

Does the moment of meaning impact the way the family worships or participates in their faith community? Is it calling them to engage in a ministry, service, or program that is new to them? Are there others in their parish who can benefit from hearing about this encounter?

As parish leaders, this is perhaps the most challenging question of the five. Here, we are challenged to create channels of influence in our programs, services, even worship, to allow for families to bring their faith encounters to—and essentially put them in dialogue with—the activities and practices of the larger community.

5. *What resources should we pursue for further growth?*

Is there a book the parent or family can read, a movie they should see, a music CD they ought to hear that will help them continue their learning and growth after this encounter? Is there a class or lecture or intergenerational event that might help? Is there a magazine or journal to which they should subscribe, or a Web site that they should frequent?

As parish leaders, we must be aware of the myriad resources available for family faith growth. And we must help families filter through all these resources so they find a good match.

The families of the four vignettes would not only benefit from pertinent resources for faith growth but, because of their encounter, they are much more likely to want to view, or read, or learn from the resource.

Spring Musical

Josh's triumph is also Mom's dream come true. She finds herself reflecting on how she has prayed for Josh continually since he was a baby. She knows that someday his talent will be discovered. In her prayer she feels a bit like the persistent widow (Luke 18:1–8) or the midnight neighbor (Luke 11:5–13) in pestering God with her prayers for her son. Now she is emboldened to ask her family to pray for Josh, and the whole cast and crew, by adding a simple blessing to their meal prayer each evening. Also, since several members of the cast and crew go to the same parish, Josh's mom asks if they could receive a special blessing on the Sunday before the show opens.

Christmas Homecoming

The day before Melissa goes back to school, she and her sister swap rooms. With their mother's guidance, they follow some purposeful steps. Before the swap, they take several pictures of each room, and recount memories of playing together in each room. After all the moving of beds, books, and clothes, the two sisters and their mom sit in each room and say a prayer of blessing.

Oregon Coast

My wife took advantage of the magical moment to start a new ritual in the family. On that trip we began a tradition of telling stories about "Jesus and his friends" at the dinner table. The idea was simple: re-tell the daily gospel story in words that our young sons could understand. They liked it, and it took. The tradition continued for years.

Taco Salad

In this instance, the connection to the sacred was not immediately apparent. Only later, upon remembering and reflecting on it, did the sacred power of the moment become evident.

Step Four: So What?

After the family has pursued the faith connection to their moment of meaning, they need to evaluate its impact. Maintaining a posture of intentional awareness, they should discuss questions such as these:

- What difference has this experience made in our lives?
- How have we grown from it?
- What about ourselves has it revealed to us?
- What memory have we created? How will we revisit it?
- What have we learned about our faith, about life, about each other?
- How will this experience change our behavior?

It is likely that individual family members will reflect on these or similar questions. Ideally, the routine of family life will bring members together for opportunities to share their reflections with each other. Of course, the family needs time and space to do this. They need plenty of quality time together in order to share with each other on a deeper level.

Spring Musical

Of course, Josh performed well, and the family has a complete video of the entire show. While Mom will never tire of watching the video, she knows Josh will grow up and move on, and his performance will seem juvenile. No matter, because she knows that for both of them this experience has renewed their confidence in God's gracious activity in their lives, and in God's response to prayer.

Christmas Homecoming

When Melissa left home the next day, she felt whole and empowered and fully loved by her family. She was glad she could give up her bedroom to her sister, but she was also glad she had a room to come home to. As she flew across the country back to school, she composed a long letter to her parents and sister thanking them for all the many gifts she had received.

Oregon Coast

The surprise trip to the Oregon Coast created a bonding and lasting memory. The memory of it is often brought up when we are all together. But from that experience we also embarked on a journey to increase our knowledge of the Bible.

Taco Salad

My involuntary remembrance of this moment is proof for me that God is active in my life and prompting me to remain on the lookout for God's grace to explode all around me. I certainly don't look at taco salad in the same way anymore.

Conclusion

I recently had a conversation with a mother whose children were in their early teens. We were discussing how important it is for parents to model and live authentic faith if they want their children to take their faith with them when they launch into young adulthood. This mother expressed a belief that no one can discern more easily than a teenager if the faith and religious practice of the child's parents and family are genuine or simply part of social adornment. I agree. And, if parents and family are genuinely pursuing their faith, then they are making efforts to connect their faith with the ordinary and extraordinary events of their daily lives.

But families need our assistance in making that connection. Most families are overwhelmed by all the information coming at them and all the expectations laid in their laps. If they perceive faith and religious practice as just one more "should" in their lives, it will likely fall near the bottom of the priority list. Yet, through the steps outlined in this chapter, they will see that their faith can actually be a valuable tool for discovering family balance, discerning choice, building camaraderie, experiencing intimacy, and, of course, growing in faith together.

Reflection Questions

1. Identify a moment of meaning in your life from which the four-step process outlined in this chapter has the potential to mine meaning.
2. Is this process similar to any others you have used? If so, which?
3. How could you share or teach this process to families, including your own?

References

Kehrwald, Leif. *Youth Ministry and Parents: Secrets for Successful Partnership.* Winona, MN: Saint Mary's Press, 2004.

Chapter Six

Family Faith & Spirituality

Kathleen Finley

Kathleen Finley is an author, speaker, and teacher in the area of practical spirituality for families and women. She also teaches in the Religious Studies Department at Gonzaga University in Spokane, Washington, and helps counsel engaged couples at her parish. She is the author or co-author of several books, including Building Christian Families *(iUniverse),* Our Family Book of Days: A Record through the Years *(Saint Mary's Press),* Welcome: Prayers for New and Pregnant Parents *(Liguori Press),* Amen: Prayers for Families with Children *(Liguori Press), and* The Liturgy of Motherhood: Moments of Grace *(Sheed and Ward). She and her husband Mitch often present together.*

EDITOR'S NOTE

Once families are able to make faith connections to the ordinary and extraordinary events of their lives, they can develop a purposeful and integrated family spirituality. In this chapter, Kathy Finley offer a vision for the domestic church rooted in the documents of Vatican II and stemming back to the early church Fathers. She also presents a myriad of practical touch points for how the parish leader can nurture the family's journey toward a vibrant spirituality through family blessings, celebrating holidays, forgiving one another, serving others, nurturing faith, and sharing meals.

Jim and Marilyn Morrison and their family are in the midst of several important spiritual experiences, though they may not realize it. Their oldest daughter is heading into adolescence and beginning to question and challenge many of her parents' ideas as she pulls away from being their little girl. The Morrisons' son is trying to understand just what it means to kind of man he admires. Their youngest daughter is rapidly leaving behind her toddler years, anticipating kindergarten and then school, where other adults, along with Marilyn and Jim, will have a major influence in her life.

The Morrisons are not that different from other families on their street, whether those families are two-parent, single-parent, or any number of other possible configurations. Change and growth occur in each household up and down their block and, for that matter, on every other street. Yet most of these families see little or no connection between what's happening in their midst and their faith lives. Why aren't they more aware of the spirituality and the holiness of what is right before their eyes?

When people take the time to reflect on their experiences they see the presence of God at work. For example, when I ask people to recall both their deepest and their greatest joy—in other words, their experiences of the cross and resurrection in their own lives—most identify events that are closely linked with their families. Family life can certainly be, to paraphrase Charles Dickens, both the best of times and the worst of times.

The home is also religiously formative. When I help new parents preparing for the sacrament of baptism to explore their role in their children's religious formation, I ask them to name what has been the most important influence on their faith. Although I am always careful to ask a "what" question, they almost always respond with a "who" answer: a parent or grandparent or teacher or some other person who has been the embodiment of God's love for them. Through their own responses, parents begin to see their potential influence on the faith lives of those with whom they live.

So, why are the Morrisons—and many of the rest of us—not more in tune with the foundational role of the spirituality that daily unfolds before us in our homes and the important impact we have on one another's faith?

One reason may be the result of the cultural divide between the secular, daily realities, and our concepts of the sacred and our religious practices—a split going back to at least the Enlightenment thinkers of the eighteenth century. We have such a different set of words and actions for each sphere of our lives—the sacred and the secular. It can seem that the world of sacraments and blessings and the world of making a living and raising a family have little to do with each other, and that the Sunday activities have little to do with the rest of the week.

We can also see some beginnings of this split when we look back to the early centuries of the Christian experience. The desert fathers and mothers headed off into remote areas of Syria and Egypt to try to live a purer, more radical form of Christianity. They were concerned that their faith seemed to be accommodating itself to the political and daily realities of life, since Christianity was no longer considered illegal. Although the faith of these early Christians had important vigor, monasticism left behind the message that those engaged in marriage and family life were somehow less holy than those willing to forsake everything to follow Jesus.

Yet faith and daily life are deeply linked. For example, the paschal mystery of the dying and rising of Christ is constantly happening in our midst, in the changes we see in the Morrison family and those that happen in the families of our parishes. Think of the daily rituals that occur in nearly every family home—sending one another forth to work or school in the morning, and blessing invoked as we tuck one another in for the night. Think of the unique customs that every family has for observing the holidays. Each family develops its own way to celebrate the holy in their midst.

There are also plenty of ways healing occurs in our homes, plenty of ways in which family members serve one another and others. These are the ways in which they share faith. Even the deceptively simple action of sharing a meal together in our homes is, in fact, a naturally eucharistic experience that has far more impact on us than we may imagine.

A Domestic Church

The daily rituals that occur in our homes happen in ways that don't look "churchy" at all; we would never think, for example, of setting up pews in the living room. But what happens within the walls of our home is no less sacred and holy than what happens within the walls of the parish church.

The early Christian community recognized this fact by calling the household the "domestic church." They use the word *ecclesia*, the Greek word for the gathering of believers, to describe the Christian household. At times they used the diminutive form of the word *ecclesiola*, or little church.

The church of the home is the most basic unit of the church, a community on which the parish and the rest of the church can be built. As the institution focused more on itself and less on its roots through the centuries, this reality was lost sight of. It was reintroduced by the Second Vatican Council in both of its documents on the church: the Dogmatic Constitution on the Church (*Lumen Gentium*) and the Pastoral Constitution on the Church in the Modern World (*Gaudium et Spes*).

In their pastoral message *Follow the Way of Love*, addressed to families on the occasion of the 1994 International Year of the Family, the U.S. bishops focus on the importance of what happens in the home. When commenting on the family as the domestic church, they say, "The point of the teaching is simple, yet profound. As Christian families, you not only belong to the Church, but your daily life is a true expression of the Church" (p. 8). After enumerating over a dozen ways in which families carry out the mission of the church in the home in ordinary ways, the bishops add this important note, which has major implications for family spirituality:

> No domestic church does all this perfectly. But neither does any parish or diocesan church. All members of the Church struggle daily to become more faithful disciples of Christ.
>
> We need to enable families to recognize that they are a domestic church. There may be families who do not understand or believe they are a domestic church. Maybe they feel overwhelmed by this calling or unable to carry out its responsibilities. Perhaps they consider their family too "broken" to be used for the Lord's purposes. But remember, a family is holy not because it is perfect but because God's grace is at work in it, helping it to set out anew everyday on the way of love. (pp. 10-11)

Perhaps the past focus on the holiness of the holy family of Jesus, Mary, and Joseph has meant that many have failed to see that all our families are holy, even though they certainly are not perfect. Another inescapable reality is that families are caught up in so much activity in their homes that it's hard to see God at work at the time. Much like Moses in Exodus, Chapter 33, people want to see God's glory, but all that God allows them to see is *God's back*—that is, to realize after the fact, when they look at the pictures or the videos, how holy their family is and how much God was in their midst.

What are some of the specific ways that families are holy, and how can parishes help families realize and celebrate that holiness more fully?

Dying and Rising

What happens in families, regardless of shape or size, is plenty of growth, which entails a constant dying and rising, a process on which we reflect especially during the season of Lent.

We saw it in several ways, for example, with the Morrisons. The oldest daughter was trying to comprehend what it meant to be an adolescent and remain a member of her family, but in a different way. Her brother was trying to understand his gender and sexual identity in a way that begins to leave his childhood behind. And their little sister was beginning to enter a world that went beyond her family at home and their influence. The parents, meanwhile, were trying to monitor these changes while attempting to meet the daily needs in their home. Families may look fairly stable, and they are in a sense, but change is also happening in their midst in small, or not-so-small, ways.

In each case, the old self is giving way in the process of change to the new life of more possibilities and new challenges. Although we rarely stop to make the connection, we are, in a very real sense, experiencing the paschal mystery, the dying and rising of Jesus that we celebrate most explicitly during Holy Week, from Holy Thursday through Good Friday to the Easter Vigil.

Those who study change tell us that the process of any life transition is one of separation, marginality, and reintegration. First is the stage of *separation*, where something outside myself brings me to a new point in my life, like being old enough for first grade, or being ready to graduate from high school, or even finding that a job is coming to an end. In each case a change is happening to me whether I want it or not.

Sometimes the initiation for change happens from within the individual, with an awareness that something ought to change. I may sense the need to look for new friends, to change the person I'm dating, or to explore new career goals. Whether the impetus comes from outside or from within, the movement is one which pulls me away from the way things have been and toward new possibilities, options that may seem unclear.

As the life change unfolds, new possibilities begin to emerge—the new school, new friend, new job, new me—but there's a sense of *marginality* that accompanies it. I'm no longer comfortable in the old reality, but I don't yet fully have my bearings in the new. I feel disoriented and uncertain, and there's a sense of risk and vulnerability with this stage. This part of my life can feel rather dark and narrow, and I'm not sure if things will ever be as clear as they once were.

In time, things begin to clear a bit, and the final stage of *reintegration* begins. I start to get my bearings and have a sense of the new me and the new possibilities in this new phase of my life. I now can see the growth that may have been happening during the uncomfortable time of marginality, even though I didn't realize it at the time. However, the relief of reintegration may be short-lived because, before long, the whole change process will happen again in a different way, not only to me but also to others in my family system.

If given the choice, we would much rather skip the separation and marginality phases—the dying aspect of the paschal mystery—and go straight to the reintegration, the resurrection, but we know in our hearts that we can't. Whether it's the hurt that follows the loss of a first love, the falling down that is part of a toddler's learning to walk, or the reality of learning to deal with the limitations of aging, we know that the cross is part of what we are called to live daily.

Not only are we faced with this reality each evening as we "die" to the day that is ending when we go to sleep and awaken to new possibilities, we also experience a bit of this dying and rising when we learn something new. We "die" to what we thought we knew so that we can "rise" to new possibilities and the power the new knowledge can give us.

How can families celebrate and ritualize this process of dying and rising, of continual separation, marginality, and reintegration in their midst? How can parishes help them appreciate the change process more fully? There are many ways that families already celebrate these small and large changes in their midst, and the parish church is already a part of many of them. But parishes can also help parents and families be more aware of what is right before them and give families the resources needed to enhance their awareness of the growth in their midst.

One way families celebrate growth and change is through birthdays. Many families have a definite ritual for celebrating a birthday. The birthday person may have certain privileges and possibilities that are not open to them the rest of the year, like choosing what to have for a birthday meal.

This is a time when families can *re-member*, recall again that we are members of one another, by pulling out some pictures of the birthday person when she or he was younger and recalling how he or she has grown. They can sing an extra verse of "Happy Birthday" ("May the good Lord bless you") as the candles on the cake are blown out. Another way some families have marked each birthday has been to assign both a new privilege and a new responsibility to mark the child's being a year older and to clearly show the link between the ability to enjoy new privileges and to share more responsibility in the household.

Some parishes acknowledge the birthdays of parish members each month and celebrate the growth in their midst by praying for them.

Whether the event is a birthday, a wedding anniversary, a graduation, a new ability or accomplishment, or a good grade, many families mark the occasion with a special dish or perhaps the use of a blessing cup to show how all our special days are important. Parishes can help families create ways to celebrate these rites of passage by providing resources for parents so families can celebrate the dying and rising in their midst. Occasional book fairs can be helpful in bringing resources to families who may not otherwise find them.

Parishes can also show families how to pray through these transition times. For example, one parish has a ritual in which teens who've recently received their driver's licenses are invited to join the presider in front of the congregation at the end of the weekend liturgy. While the new drivers hold their keys high, the congregation extends their hands and prays for wisdom and safety as these young people gain a new responsibility. The simple ceremony ends with the pastor giving them special key rings from the parish community.

In a parish, however, it can be easy to overlook the more difficult and major challenges that many families face: challenges of addiction and recovery, depression or other mental illnesses, eating disorders, domestic violence, divorce, unemployment, disability, aging, and loneliness. Addressing these issues in parish programs and including these topics occasionally in homilies may help families facing these challenges feel less alone. They may also begin to feel more able to come forward for the help they need, knowing that these problems are part of the way God is present in their midst, though hidden at times.

Another way parishes can help families deal with the paschal mystery, the dying and rising that is associated with change in their homes, is to emphasize the community dimension to every growth point in the parish. Parents need to be involved with sacramental preparation, whether it's baptism, first Eucharist, or confirmation. Parents and other family members can also be invited to a gathering that helps them understand the spiritual growth that is happening to a family member, whether it is a young person or an adult coming back from a powerful retreat experience, or any other activity that helps his or her faith grow, such as the Rite of Christian Initiation of Adults. In this way, other family members can help support the new growth instead of resisting it out of a lack of awareness.

The more the parish is aware of and acknowledges the fundamental holiness of what happens at home and in the family community, the more it can successfully build on what occurs there and help the members of those domestic churches understand and celebrate the constant changes.

Many ethnic traditions can help amplify the communal dimension of family rites of passage, from the Hispanic tradition in some places of *padrinos* (couple sponsors) for a marriage, to the various traditions surrounding the funeral or wake for a family member. Most parish communities do a wonderful job of accompanying families as they face challenges from cradle to grave, and the more parishioners see themselves as a resource to the primary community of faith in the home, the more helpful they will be.

Family Blessings

A helpful starting place to build an awareness of the natural sacredness of families and practical ways to enhance and celebrate that reality is with parents preparing for their child's baptism. These parents are quite aware of the holiness of their new child and are eager for suggestions for sharing faith with their children. Some of the parents may be familiar with the custom of a nightly blessing for their children, but many are not.

Although as Catholics we may tend to think of the priest as the one who blesses, parents are more than qualified to bless their children. After demonstrating how my husband and I would bless our children when they were small, I usually ask the participants in a session to bless one another so they get some hands-on practice of how to do this. The exact words and actions may vary from one family to another—as does each family's unique spirituality—but often the nightly blessing involve a sign of the cross traced on the child's forehead and a prayer of God's blessing and keeping that child safe and giving him or her a peaceful night.

This ritual combines feeling tucked in and naturally reflective at the end of the day with being secure in the love and care of God and one's parents. The parents from whom we learned this ritual said that their oldest son returned from the Marines and asked for his father's blessing, something he'd missed while he was gone. That's how powerful family rituals like this can be.

Yet any family ritual has to evolve as a family changes. When our sons began to have messier rooms than I was comfortable with, I explained that I couldn't come in to give a nightly blessing because I might turn my ankle. No problem, my oldest son assured me; he came out of his room to receive the blessing and then went back into his cluttered room.

Blessings can be used for many other times in a family's life. Some families use them each morning as everyone leaves for work or school. Our family never got that organized every morning, but we did use blessings before any of us went on a trip. When our children were small, it was usually my husband and I who were leaving them with a sitter, and they who blessed us to keep us safe on our travels. As our sons grew older, the blessings changed a bit, sometimes sounding like "May the Force be with you," so that they could still continue our family ritual and yet be "cool" as well.

The ways that blessings can be used in a family are as endless as the occasions that arise within a family: birthdays, a good report card, preparation for a big test or game, celebrating a new driver, anticipating the prom, and even heading off to college. When a parent gives their child a blessing, that parent knows that God's love as well as his or hers goes with that child in a special way into whatever the child will face.

Parish communities can model family blessings by having commissioning services for those involved in special ministries within the parish, or for those with special needs (e.g., those preparing for marriage or those expecting a child). The events that will be significant may vary somewhat from one parish to another. A parish in a particularly mobile area may conduct a regular blessing for those who are moving. In a parish with many young adults, blessings may be helpful for those going off to military service or volunteer work, if such a practice is appropriate.

Celebrating Holidays

Although some families may not give one another blessings, the spirituality of every family is quite evident, especially to an outsider, in the ways in which they celebrate holidays. Many families have a central gathering place for holiday times, perhaps the grandparents' home or the house of someone who is more centrally located. Some families make it a point to get away to a resort or an out-of-the-way spot so they can focus on each other more than on other influences such as TV or video games or presents. More important than where the family gathers, of course, is what they do when they are together.

Each term I have my college students describe a ritual in their family. The descriptions vary widely. Some can tell me exactly what the menu will be for a particular holiday and who will fix what and how every part of the day will go: Aunt Clara will bring her special relish or her favorite dessert and then Uncle George will have to do his traditional toast. Some family gatherings and traditions may be explicitly religious, and some less so.

Other families have devised unique rituals, like the family that was largely made up of engineers who loved getting the "tree" to put up on Christmas Eve. Finding the tree consisted of locating the straightest, tallest trunk they could find on their property; then enhancing it by drilling the trunk at key places; and filling the drilled holes in with branches from the fullest, shorter trees they could find. The result was a "super tree," as unique in all the world as is their ritual of tree cutting and building to provide their main decoration for the Christmas season.

A family may not realize how strong their traditions are, mainly because these patterns are so expected that they don't need to be discussed or even thought about. But a visitor who is unfamiliar with them, especially one who may be joining the family by marriage, will quickly learn what "we always do," whether it's for Christmas or Easter, the Fourth of July or Thanksgiving Day. These rituals and traditions may grow and change as the family does, but many families would not think of missing one of their family gatherings because they know how important the link with one another is in the midst of a busy world.

If we want to know anything about the importance of rituals, the ones to consult are the toddlers. Ask a four-year-old what the ritual is for bedtime so that a new sitter knows the "drill," and you'll find out that there is a definite "way things are done" so that all is well.

One of our sons helped remind me of the importance of traditions and rituals by his unexpected questions just as he was entering adolescence. Here was a young man who had declared himself no longer interested in church or religion; but he was also asking me in early November if I had everything I needed for making the Advent wreath and when would we be hanging the Christmas stockings on our fireplace. When I stopped to reflect on it, I realized that almost everything in his world was in the process of changing and was swirling around him in those years. He needed to know that there were things that remained the same this year as they were last year and as they would be next year. This is what rituals do for us: they remind us of who we truly are in the midst of so much change.

Parishes can help families be more aware of the traditions they already have and enhance these rituals with new possibilities, such as the Advent wreath and a nativity scene or daily prayer and the rice bowl for the poor during Lent. One way to do this is to have an Advent or Lent Fair where families can share what has worked for them, and together make an

Advent wreath or a Lenten cross for use at home. Perhaps the parish newsletter or bulletin can occasionally feature a family from the parish and the ways they celebrate a certain season together to give other families ideas on how they can share their own unique rituals.

Healing and Forgiveness

There is much need for healing and forgiveness in family life. We are far from perfect in our dealings with others, especially those with whom we live. We are not patient enough, not affirming enough, and often too short on time to spend some with another, to just listen and be with each other.

Only in considering the example of God's unconditional love for each and every person can families find ways to forgive each other's failures.

When our middle son and I would butt heads—which was often because we were stubborn—we always agreed at the end of the day that, although we might sorely disagree with each other, the love is always stronger than the hurt. That ability to know that we are held in love—for one another and in God—is the grace that can happen daily in families.

Parishes can help affirm and encourage families to be aware of the process of forgiveness and reconciliation in their midst and to remember, as the U.S. bishops pointed out in the pastoral letter *Follow the Way of Love*, that families are holy not because they are perfect but because God's grace is at work in them.

Parents, for example, are doing far more than they may realize to help prepare their children for the sacrament of reconciliation by not only having them ask forgiveness of one another, but also by asking forgiveness of their children when appropriate. Just listening to and caring for one another is a source of healing, a way in which family members wash each other's feet. There are countless ways that families kiss one another's "owies."

Parishes can help families acknowledge and communicate the ways that they hurt one another and need each other's forgiveness, especially in anticipation of a parish reconciliation service or before the reception of First Reconciliation. Parishes can distribute "I'm sorry" notes to be filled in by family members and then given to one another to help ritualize the need for mutual reconciliation.

Serving Others

There is plenty of serving one another within families and by families toward others. Much goes unnoticed. It's just "what needs to be done":

laundry, grocery shopping, cleaning—the list is endless. As family members grow they are expected to help assume these responsibilities, and in so doing they are feeding the hungry, clothing the naked, and so on. They may not think that doing laundry and fixing meals are parts of the spiritual and corporal works of mercy, but they are doing these things for the least of their brothers and sisters as Jesus commanded.

Families also find themselves caring for others outside the family circle, whether helping an elderly neighbor with yard work, gathering food for the local food bank, or collecting pledges and walking or running for a favorite charity. These acts of service accomplish at least two things for the family members involved: they provide opportunity for family members to put their faith and their care for others into action, and they expand peoples' imagination and empathy regarding how it might feel to be in someone else's shoes.

Parishes can help support families in acts of service by providing or publicizing various opportunities for service, such as the Interfaith Hospitality Network for homeless families, Meals on Wheels, or a local women's shelter. Parishes can also help acknowledge those who serve within the parish as well as outside it, so that others can see how important a life of service is. (See Chapter Nine for more ideas.)

Nurturing Faith

In the midst of the dying and rising, giving blessings, celebrating holidays, sharing forgiveness and healing, and serving others, family members grow in faith. This sharing of faith does not take the place of formal catechesis, but it complements it, applying it to the real events that are right before the family's eyes.

For example, a death in the family brings with it the opportunity to talk about life after death, and how this family member is with God and happy in a way they can only imagine. If the person who has died was young, had suffered a great deal, or possibly committed suicide, this fact raises still other issues: how can God be loving and yet allow this to happen? A family member with a disability or who is aging may raise issues about respect for life at all stages of the life cycle. Events on television or in a movie or perhaps at work or school can stir up plenty of moral questions: what would you do in a situation like that? What do you think Jesus would have done, and why?

Through the bulletin and homilies, parishes can suggest topics for families to talk about at times related to the liturgical year. For example, the feasts of All Saints and All Souls invite a family to explore who they know who might be considered a saint, and to talk about the communion of saints. The feast of Corpus Christi or the occasion of First Eucharist in the parish gives families an opportunity to talk about how they understand the Eucharist in their lives. The Easter Vigil or other times of baptism give them the opportunity to talk about the sacrament and what it means to them. Perhaps they will also tell some stories about the baptisms of family members.

Sharing a Meal

Yet another way that God is evident in the home is when the family gathers for the important ritual of sharing a meal. When families gather, they bring more than physical hunger to the table; they bring the desire to be fed by the presence of and interaction with one another. This is far more than the refueling stop that some of the commercials for fast-food chains would have them believe.

And somehow families know that this is a holy experience. When I ask parents what they would say is the holiest place in their home, most will answer the family table, the place where they most often gather together.

But we also need to acknowledge that there are plenty of predators for the endangered species that is the family meal. The schedules that families keep, especially for the children, are overfilled. Preparation time to make healthy meals is virtually nonexistent. Distractions via media and electronic gadgets abound. The television is a not-so-invited "guest" each evening in the homes of about half of the families that do have dinner together, usually monopolizing the "conversation" with the nightly news.

Even though we live in a culture that continues to erode both the importance and the possibility of a shared meal, we are also beginning to realize its value. I am convinced that children coming from homes with regular family meals tend to have better grades and better manners than do those from families in which everyone eats on the run.

Although our culture may not be supportive of sharing meals, the parish can help encourage families in this regard with ideas and suggestions for meal prayers and conversations during certain times of the year. The parish can suggest being intentional about the family meal as an important ritual during the season of Lent, leading up to Holy Thursday. This is appropriate because each meal is naturally eucharistic—even if it's boring leftovers. When we share ourselves and our food, not only are we companions—literally those who share bread (*pane*) with (*cum*) one another—but we also experience Christ's presence in our midst, as he promised when he said that when two or more are gathered in his name he would be there with us.

Sharing a meal is an experience that helps prepare children for Eucharist as well. Carol Luebering, in her helpful booklet *Your Child's First Communion*, emphasizes that the stage has been set long before the child goes up to receive the host for the first time. She reminds parents that the process of feeding their little ones—first in their arms and then in a high chair before "graduating" to the stage when the child sits as a full member at the table—has a parallel in faith. The parents have helped nurture the child's growth in faith in many ways, making it possible for the child to take a full role at the table of the Lord in the midst of the parish community. Yes, far more is happening at a family meal than meets the eye.

Parishes can help encourage families to say grace together as they begin a meal and to take time to share the highs and lows of each person's day. This is a good way to encourage reflection and shared intimacy within the family that will pay off for years to come.

Of course, Eucharist isn't the only sacrament that begins at home. Every day in these homes washing, bathing, even anointing occurs that echo the sacraments of baptism, confirmation, and anointing of the sick. Every day in these homes, the hungry are fed, the naked are clothed, and the sick are visited and ministered to.

As they look more carefully and more reflectively, the Morrison family, and the rest of us, will see more and more ways in which God is present, hidden in the midst of much that looks quite ordinary. With help and encouragement from their parish faith communities they can see Christ present among them when they share simple things like being aware of the dying and rising in their midst, blessing one another, celebrating holidays, forgiving one another, serving others, talking about their faith, and sharing a meal together.

Reflection Questions

1. The church teaches that the family is the domestic church. Do you think we as church are reflecting this teaching in our interactions with families? Why or why not?

2. Read the statement below. How do you feel about the help and encouragement your community offers families? Are you hopeful about what can be done, or does it seem impossible?

> With help and encouragement from their parish faith communities they can see Christ present among them when they share simple things like being aware of the dying and rising in their midst, blessing one another, celebrating holidays, forgiving one another, serving others, talking about their faith, and sharing a meal together.

References

U.S. Catholic Bishops. *Follow the Way of Love*. Washington, DC: United States Catholic Conference, 1994.

Chapter Seven

Families & Christian Practice

Leif Kehrwald
(See bio on page 26)

EDITOR'S NOTE

Once families are able to make faith connections to the ordinary and extraordinary events of their lives, they can develop a purposeful and integrated family spirituality. In this chapter, Kathy Finley offer a vision for the domestic church rooted in the documents of Vatican II and stemming back to the early church Fathers. She also presents a myriad of practical touch points for how the parish leader can nurture the family's journey toward a vibrant spirituality through family blessings, celebrating holidays, forgiving one another, serving others, nurturing faith, and sharing meals.

Families grow in faith when given opportunities and encouragement to practice faith in concrete ways: faith conversation, ritual and celebration, scripture study and reflection, prayer, outreach, and service for others. From the time my sons learned to speak they have been afflicted with the condition I have since come to call "passive irresponsibility." Whenever anything goes awry, they always come up with a perfectly passive response. They have a knack for putting action and responsibility on things that cannot possibly take action or responsibility.

A couple of examples will illustrate. One day, at the age of six or so, my son asked, "Dad, when will the dime that fell down my throat come out?" Notice how he placed all the action, and therefore blame, on the dime. He took no responsibility for swallowing it.

What is a parent to say? Surely it will pass.

My other son demonstrated the same affliction one Summer day when I came upon him changing his shorts in the middle of the day. "What are you doing?" I asked. "Dad, my underpants got peed on." There was nobody else around, so you would think he would own that action. But no. Passive irresponsibility lets him off the hook.

It is normal for young children to take a somewhat passive approach to much of life simply because they have little or no control over many of their experiences. It's challenging for children to figure out what they can and cannot control. Yet, developmentally, as children grow and mature, they must take a more active responsibility for his or her choices.

What does this story of passive irresponsibility have to do with family life and faith development? Many families, while quite deliberate and intentional about many areas of their life, tend to take a rather passive approach toward their own faith growth. It's not that they don't care about faith, but many seem content and complacent about turning over the role of faith leader to the local parish faith formation program.

Many of these same families would never consider abrogating their childcare, health care, athletic, or even academic responsibilities in the same way. In these arenas, many parents and families demand an active role and a working partnership with the institutions providing these services. Yet with respect to the faith formation, many parents take a passive approach and leave their children with the catechist or religion teacher hoping for the best. I contend that this posture has been reinforced by church leadership through subtle messages that faith growth takes place primarily, if not exclusively, on church grounds.

Intention

God's grace is so awesome and plentiful that every so often it explodes in our faces, unannounced and unanticipated. It's a pure gift reflecting God's unconditional and unfailing love for all. Just about anyone can tell you about an experience or two of such grace. Yet because of human weakness, we tend to count on those occasional bursts of grace to see us through the tough times and unexpected challenges of life (passive). Further, we tend to expect those random acts of gifted grace to be well-timed in accordance our serious struggles and disasters (passive irresponsibility).

The message of this chapter can be captured in a single word: intention. The opposite of passive is active. The opposite of passive irresponsibility is deliberate intention. Our Christian heritage and theology have always recognized the necessity for intention with respect to faith. Belief in God is not a passive enterprise. It is active and intentional. In my book *Youth Ministry and Parents*, I wrote that while God's grace is offered unconditionally and without price, Christians have always believed that personal faith is required for the grace to be fully received. This is the essence of human freedom and relational theology. Emerging from this theology is the important notion of Christian practice. What are the things Christian believers do intentionally to seek and receive God's free gift of grace? A key to family faith development is families choosing to engage in the practices and activities that enrich their well-being and enhance their faith. These practices are both innovative and rich with tradition, and they are always life-giving. (pp. 94-95)

The challenge for parish leaders is to assist families in the transition from passive irresponsibility to active responsibility. No small task!

What Is Meant by Christian Practice?

In *Practicing Our Faith*, Dorothy Bass offers a straightforward definition of Christian practice. "Christian practices are things Christian people do together over time in response to and in light of God's active presence for the life of the world" (p. 5). She also notes that practices address fundamental human needs and conditions through concrete human acts (p. 6).

This implies an inherent practicality to the things Christians do. To be holy doesn't necessarily mean lofty, mysterious, transcendent-like angelic activity. Perhaps the most sacred thing families can do is simply be family as best they can. This then implies a strong connection between basic human needs and spiritual faith needs. They are not so separate as some tend to think.

Bass puts it this way: "Practices, therefore, have practical purposes: to heal, to shape communities, to discern. Oddly, however, they are not treasured only for their outcomes. Just taking a full and earnest part in them is somehow good in itself" (p. 7). The merit of Christian practices is not solely based on results. Often we cannot know the results, but we know that the practices are good, and that is reason enough to do them.

Practices are done together over time. One must seek just the right balance between tradition and innovation, recognizing that neither is helpful without genuine meaning. Just because we've always done it that way doesn't make it worthwhile. Likewise, change for change's sake is seldom helpful. Effective Christian practice brings a healthy blend of traditional thinking and fresh insights.

Practices possess standards of excellence. We need to be prepared to think about what it means to do them well rather than badly. Sincerity, effort, and right intention are indeed very important but not enough by themselves. Practice is concrete and practical, and therefore must be done well. When a young musician prepares for his recital, he is expected to master certain skills and to be able to perform them. Therefore, he practices his piece over and over.

Like a physician who practices medicine, or an attorney who practices law, Christians are called to practice their faith. "Through Christian practices, we come to perceive how our daily lives are all tangled up with the things God is doing in the world. Now we want to figure out how to pattern our practices after God's, and it becomes our deepest hope to become partners in God's reconciling love for the world" (p. 8).

One more thing about practices: they are all interrelated. They flow into one another, each one making a space for God's active presence that then ripples into other parts of life.

Intentional Christian Practice and Family Life

How can one put these challenges into practical language and doable activities that a family can grasp? In many respects, it all comes down to discipleship: the family chooses to *intentionally* live as disciples of Jesus as a household. How does a family exercise discipleship? How do they live the ordinary and extraordinary events of their lives in a way that reflects their beliefs in Jesus? Consider the characteristics of family discipleship. You have permission to reproduce these points and give them to families.

Characteristics of Family Discipleship

Call. As a family, we not only sense God's presence in our life, but also a mission and call to place ourselves at God's disposal in some way, however minor or major.

Commitment. We make a promise of faithfulness to God and each other. We pledge to support each other and lift each other up when individual commitments are waning.

Values. Our decisions are rooted in core Christian values such as compassion, love, self-sacrifice, and community. When confronted with choices, big or small, we filter them through our values and try to make the best possible choice.

Trust. We place our life in God's and in each other's hands. We don't look for a way out of the hard times, rather, we look for God's guidance and support through them. We also pledge to be there for each other—over and over again.

Practice. Like the attorney who practices law and the physician who practices medicine, we practice our faith. We express ourselves as believers without apology or embarrassment, yet we never flaunt or condescend.

Discipline. We stay the course of our beliefs even when the good times seem to have abandoned us. God is more than a feeling or an urge to be satisfied. We seek to live our faith, even when we would prefer to do otherwise.

Prayer, Ritual, and Worship. As Jesus' disciples, we seek to connect with him. We pray together at home; we pray for each other in our solitude; we ritualize the key moments of change in our family life; we regularly worship with the larger community of believers.

Service, Compassion, and Generosity toward Others. We never forget that no matter how trying times may be, there are always others who are less fortunate than ourselves. Discipleship calls us out of our own woes and into works of mercy and justice for others. Ironically, these works often have great healing power in our own family.

Communion. We recognize that discipleship is not a solitary journey, and so we seek to connect with others who share our convictions. Christianity is a communal faith. Each one of us holds pearls of grace that must be shared with all.

Reflection. We take moments to look back on our day, our week, our year, our key events to see if we can discern God's gracious activity in our lives. There is no question that God is present among us, but we must set aside time to reflect on it.

(*Youth Ministry and Parents*, pp. 96-99, adapted)

The theology and tradition of Christian practice and its particular challenge for families is also supported by reputable research. Recent data among Christians in general and Catholics in particular shows that parents and families play an increasingly important role in the faith formation and development of their children. Furthermore, certain activities and practices engaged in at home in a family setting are crucial to the faith development of young people.

In my conversations with catechetical leaders all across the country, the one consistent message that I hear from all is simply this: our traditional catechetical process of 60-90 minutes in age-specific classrooms once a week with a volunteer catechist, *all by itself,* isn't working. The way we have done faith formation, all by itself, just isn't getting the job done. However, the research described below points to a partnership between the parish and the home that indicates more positive results are possible. (*Youth Ministry and Parents,* p. 100)

The partnership begins with the parish leader. Many parishes have made a significant shift in the manner and method of faith formation they provide to parishioners. They have shifted from a child-focused, age-segmented, textbook-driven program to a process of faith formation for all ages, centered around the events of the life of the community, and conducted primarily in intergenerational settings. See *Generations of Faith Resource Manual* for a full introduction for this process.

In *Youth Ministry and Parents,* I describe in detail some of the research on families and religious practice.

> On the home front, parents and families also play a key role. In their book, *The Search for Common Ground: What Unites and Divides Catholic Americans,* James Davidson and his Purdue University colleagues found family religious practice to be a key predictor of one's adult faith practice. This book reports the conclusions from a rather extensive study of the beliefs and religious activity of currently practicing, as well as nonpracticing Catholics. Catholic parishioners were surveyed from throughout the U.S., and interviewed from across the state of Indiana. Generally, the research highlights the importance of certain factors in establishing an adult commitment to faith. These factors point toward pastoral initiatives, such as fostering a healthy home life, early childhood experiences, and a good religious education.
>
> With respect to family and parental influence, some of the specific results showed…
>
> Family upbringing variables have a strong effect on the respondents' tendency, as adults, to accept traditional Catholic beliefs and practices and to agree with the Church on sexual and reproductive ethics. The strongest predictor of a high score on both of these indices is the respondent's level of childhood religiosity: respondents who report frequent Mass attendance, Communion, and prayer as children are over eight times more likely to report high levels of traditional beliefs and practices today. (p. 98)
>
> Respondents who were close to their parents or whose parents frequently talked to them about religion are twice as likely to report high levels of traditional beliefs and practices than those who were not close to their parents or whose parents "rarely" or "never" talked about religion. (pp. 98-99)
>
> The factor with the most impact on Catholics' religious beliefs and practices is childhood religiosity—nurtured through the family and parish or school religious education. (pp. 100-101)

Family influences are extremely important, especially when parents talk about religion with their children. It seems that remaining active in one's childhood church is more attractive to those with strong family connections. Childhood religiosity affects closeness to God. The more people learn to be religious as children, the more likely they are to report experiences of the holy later in life. In other words, the way young people are raised has long-term effects on their ability to experience God in their adult years. Childhood religiosity also fosters commitment to the church. Catholics who learn to be religious when they are young find it relatively easy to claim their Catholic identity. They also come to appreciate the benefits of being Catholic.

> The Davidson study is corroborated by a Search Institute study which found that the three most important factors that empower the faith maturity among young people are all family-based. What do we mean by "faith maturity"? It is a young person's ability to say "yes" to her beliefs, own them to herself, and act on them by her own choice.
>
> But the research shows that without key formative experiences in the home, genuine faith maturity is harder to come by. What are these formative experiences? There are three.
>
> *Family Faith Conversations.* Hearing their parents' faith stories is one of the most important influences on the faith of children and teenagers. Open-ended discussions on relevant and controversial issues create an atmosphere for dialogue and growth. While it's important for parents to know just how they stand on a given issue, it's just as important to allow for a variety of opinions. It's also helpful when parents are willing to share about times of doubt and questioning in their own faith journey. Sharing the rough points can create new opportunities for conversation and understanding.
>
> *Family Ritual and Devotion.* This activity moves from informal conversation to something a bit more structured and intentional. People who regularly have family devotions, prayer, or Bible reading at home tend to have higher faith maturity.
>
> Do you know the difference between habit and ritual? Reflection. Families who take some time to reflect on their daily, weekly, and seasonal habits, will likely discover some opportunities for family ritual.
>
> *Family Outreach and Service.* Faced with so many problems of their own, many families are not motivated to serve others. Yet often, acts of selfless mercy can transform woes into healing and bring help to those in greater need. There is no more powerful influence of faith and family unity than working together to help others. One sure way to gain a world vision and a desire to serve others is to invite people who represent issues in the world to come visit and perhaps share a meal. (pp. 101-102)

This research points to several concrete practices that believing families can engage in that greatly enhances the likelihood that children will grow up as active believers, choose to live faith-full lives as young adults and grow in their own Christian practices. There is no guarantee, of course, but these activities greatly increase the odds.

Helpful Suggestions

In my own work with groups of parents and families, I try to offer practical suggestions and give helpful resources for engaging in these activities.

Family Faith Conversations

- Take advantage of teachable moments. The more in touch we are with our own faith journey, the fewer teachable moments will escape us.
- Take time to listen and share. What is the "talkative" time of day for your child?
- Invite discussion on a provocative issue or controversial topic.
- Allow doubts and different opinions to be expressed.
- Be willing to be questioned about your own views and beliefs.
- Take opportunities to pray together.
- Use Scripture as a source for discussing an issue.
- Set up a one-to-one time with each child. Build personal memories together.
- Use media (TV, radio, computer, etc.) and current events as discussion starters. "What do you think of online pornography as it relates to censorship and free speech?"
- Tell or read stories together.

Family Ritual and Devotion

- Tell stories of "Jesus and His Friends"
- Give simple blessings to each other and the things we use daily: bikes, school supplies, etc.
- Initiate at least one annual religious ritual in your family each year.
- Rediscover and retain the ethnic religious traditions that are your legacy.
- Give your family rituals time, space, and planning.
- Get a book or two on family prayer and ritual.
- Share responsibility for celebration and ritual among all family members.
- Adopt the attitude: If it's worth doing, it's worth doing to the best of your ability! Even if we're not very good at doing ritual, it still has a powerful impact.

- Try this simple exchange when leaving the house in the morning.
  Parent: This is the day the Lord has made.
  Child: I will rejoice and be glad.
- Set up a regular time for family prayer, e.g. Tuesday night family prayer. The family member in charge can lead the prayer however he or she wishes, and at the end select next week's leader.
- Do seasonal rituals: Advent, Lent, Easter, etc.
- Celebrate baptism days as well as birthdays. Light the child's baptismal candle and tell the story of his or her birth and baptism.

Family Outreach and Service
- Regularly invite children to join in social action. Be inviting without inflicting guilt.
- Expose children to advocates, victims, and their situations. Diffuse their fear and ignorance.
- Actions should be within children's capacities. Look for opportunities in which children can play a specific role; respect their limits.
- Integrate fun whenever possible. Combine the action with a fun event. Join with other families.
- Do "with" instead of do "for." Respect and promote the dignity of others. Learn from those you hope to serve.
- Consider both works of justice and works of mercy. In addition to caring for victims, work to change systems that victimize them.
- Once a month deliver food to needy families via St. Vincent de Paul Society.
- Help serve in a soup kitchen.
- Commit yourselves to visiting an elderly person on a regular basis.
- Volunteer with Habitat for Humanity
- Take part in donation efforts for re-useable clothing and other items.
- Participate in Save a Family Plan to support a poor family in India.

There are many additional ideas, activities, and resources available. With a list such as this, I often invite parents to discuss with each other the activities they already do and which ones they might want to try. Then, I invite them to reflect and converse as a family, using the following questions.
- What is one immediate step your family can take to incorporate some of these faith-building activities?
- Name one long-term goal your family can set in order to grow in faith.

Conclusion

The family is a domestic church, a church of the home. The family is called to engage in traditional Christian practices that truly nurture the church of the home. It is in the bosom of the family that parents are "by word and example...the first heralds of the faith with regard to their children. They should encourage them in the vocation which is proper to each child" (LG 11).

At the moment we claim what the Christian family is—domestic church—we are immediately confronted with the question: What does the Christian family do? Therefore, we describe the ancient and traditional practices of living the Christian life...in a family way.

Reflection Questions

1. Ponder this statement: "But the research shows that without key formative experiences *in the home*, genuine faith maturity is harder to come by." What power do you as a leader possess to impact faith practice in the home?
2. When you think of your own family, what practices nurtured or continue to nurture your faith?

References

Bass, Dorothy C., editor. *Practicing Our Faith: A Way of Life for a Searching People*. San Francisco: Jossey-Bass Publishers, 1997.

Catechism of the Catholic Church. Washington, DC: United States Catholic Conference, 1997.

Davidson, James, et al. *The Search for Common Ground: What Unites and Divides Catholic Americans*. Huntington, IN: Our Sunday Visitor, 1997.

Flannery, Austin, O.P. *Vatican Council II: The Conciliar and Post-Conciliar Documents*. New York: Costello Publishing, 1975.

Roehlkepartain, Eugene C. *The Teaching Church: Moving Christian Education to Center Stage*. Nashville, TN: Abingdon Press, 1993.

Chapter Eight

Families & Worship

Judith Dunlap

*Judith Dunlap has been involved in religious educa-
tion for almost thirty years. She is the author of
Practical Catechesis: Visions and Tasks for
Religious Educators, When You Are a
Catechist, and When You Teach In a Catholic
School, and coauthored God Is Calling, a family catechetical series. Judith has a MA in theology
and a BA in education. She chaired the
Catechetical Renewal Network for ten years, wrote
the religious education column for CHURCH
magazine for nine years, and has given workshops
and retreats across the country. Presently, Judith is
working as a catechetical consultant for St.
Anthony Messenger Press & Franciscan
Communications. She is a wife and mother of five
adult children, grandmother of six.*

EDITOR'S NOTE

Perhaps the most important component of lifelong catechesis for the whole community is drawing a connection between what the community learns and how the community worships. For families, worship is the most crucial Christian practice, yet fewer and fewer families worship regularly. In this chapter, Judith Dunlap shows how families can incorporate Catholic worship into the rhythm of their lives, integrating the church year feasts, seasons, and sacraments with seasons and patterns of family living.

Standing on my bookcase is a framed photo of our family taken at a parish family retreat many years ago. The frame is made in the shape of a triangle with Popsicle® sticks and has a toothpick cross on top. On the bottom of the triangle frame are the words, "We are church." Every time I look at it I remember that weekend and the fun we had playing and praying together. Fifteen years and six grandchildren later, we all look a lot different, but love still calls us together to play and pray. Whether all seventeen are together, or just two of us around the table, that framed picture reminds me that we are church.

The word "church" is a translation of the Greek word *ekklesia*, which means "an assembly of those called out." Early Christians chose this word to describe their assembly because they saw themselves as called by God. We, too, are that assembly. God called us, and we answered. Whenever, wherever we gather in response to that call, we are church.

The number gathered is not important because the church is not the sum total of all her members. Each community, no matter how small, is church. The place it gathers is even less important. Most of us gather on Sundays to worship together in parish churches, but little churches gather regularly around a kitchen table.

As we read in Chapter Six, the Christian family has been called the little church or domestic church from the early centuries. The documents of Vatican II remind us of this distinction. In *Decree on the Apostolate of the Laity* we are told that the family becomes the domestic sanctuary of the church when its members love each other, when they pray and serve together, and when the "whole family makes itself a part of the liturgical worship of the church" (*Apostolicam Actuositatem* 11).

The family is church whenever, wherever it gathers in response to God's call. And like larger congregational churches, how the family responds to the call is a clear reflection of its understanding of God. How family members pray, learn, reconcile, play, and serve can tell us something about their self-image and their image of God. How a church, congregational or domestic, worships is a similar barometer.

How Catholics Worship

I remember the first time I became aware of the uniqueness of Catholic worship. It was my first year of college and I had invited a non-Catholic friend to Christmas midnight Mass. Afterward, I spent the car trip home trying to answer his questions. Why do you sit, stand, and kneel so much? What was that spicy smelling smoke they kept waving around? Do you really believe Jesus is in that wafer and wine the priest held up?

I answered as best I could, but most of my responses were no more than a phrase or two. Today, several sacramental theology courses later, I would answer very differently. It would take more than a car trip home to explain all the reasons Catholics move around so much, use incense, or believe in the Real Presence. I would have to begin by explaining a Catholic's understanding of who God is, who we are, and how God relates to us.

Catholics believe in a triune God whom we call Father, Son, Spirit. The Father, our creator, is the source of all life and is infinitely good. All of creation embodies that goodness. The Son, Jesus our brother, shares our humanity so that we can share in his divinity. He is the Word with us from the beginning, the Way, the Truth, and the Life. The Spirit, our sanctifier, brings us together, highlighting our gifts and strengthening our weaknesses. The spirit draws us into the dynamic embrace of love that is the triune God.

We believe that the Incarnation means that God, in the person of Jesus, not only walked the earth 2,000 years ago, but is also with us today. In fact, Christ is not just with us, Christ is in us, and in all of creation, in friend and foe, in blades of grass and summer storms, in oil and water and bread and wine. For Catholics, all worship is through Christ, with Christ, and in Christ, in the unity of the Holy Spirit.

We see ourselves as children of God, exceedingly grateful for the eternal love and life that God shares with us. We are the body of Christ willing to be broken and shared with the world. We are empowered by the Spirit to share God's love and life wherever we go.

We are aware of our limitations: we know that God is beyond our comprehension and that any understanding we have of God is insufficient. We learn about God as we learn about everything else, through our five senses, as well as our intuitive sense. Yet each of us experiences God differently. We can read the same Bible, hear the same sermon, see the same sunset, but the experience of finding God in what we see, hear, smell, touch, or taste is colored by our individual life experiences and tinted by our own intuitive perception. Experiencing God is always deeply personal.

It is an experience beyond our ability to communicate or duplicate, and yet the very nature of the Christ experience demands that we respond by sharing and celebrating the gift we have received. So we use metaphors and symbols, and we try to create an environment complimentary to the experience so that the deeply personal can be celebrated in the only appropriate way, through thanksgiving and praise in community.

This communal prayer and public response is worship. Worship is an expression of our relationship with God. Catholics celebrate God the same way we learn about God, through our limited senses and intuitive perception. We use symbols like words, actions, and concrete signs—such as water, bread, and wine and oil—but we also rely on experiences more inherent to the imageless nature of God like color and form, rhythm and tension.

God does not need the incense, candles, beautiful music, colorful fabrics, or even the blessed bread and wine. We offer these fine things because they are the best we can provide to express our love. Even more importantly, we need them, along with the meaningful rituals that capsulate them, to remind ourselves of our collective experience of Christ.

All of this is liturgy, the primary way Catholics worship publicly (see *Catechism of the Catholic Church* #1070). In our Catholic tradition, liturgy includes the sacraments, the Liturgy of Hours, and, above all else, the Eucharist. We will look at each of these worship experiences and discuss how we can help families celebrate them more fully with the parish, and prepare for and continue to celebrate them at home.

The Eucharist

In his book *Sacraments: How Catholics Pray*, Rev. Thomas Richstatter, OFM, reminds us that the Eucharist is the first sacrament, and *the* sacrament. It is the one all the other sacraments are modeled after. He tells us that the Eucharist "contains all that we are, all that the church is, all that Jesus says of God" (p. 51).

Hopefully, by looking briefly at the Eucharist from different vantage points, we can find a variety of ways to help families experience this great sacrament and experience the gifts of Eucharist at home. We will look at five aspects of the sacrament: Eucharist as story; Eucharist as sacrifice; Eucharist as meal; the Real Presence; and the Liturgical Year.

Eucharist as Story

In the Eucharist, God calls us in love and we respond in love. After the introductory rite we enter into the Liturgy of the Word. The readings from Scripture are God's self-revelation, his loving call inviting us into relationship. The homily relates the readings to our everyday lives, showing us how God is calling us today.

Make sure parents understand how important it is to help their children get to know God—particularly Jesus—through the Scriptures. If the parish is financially able, give each family a family Bible or a children's Bible. Encourage parents to read the stories in sequence so that their children will begin to have a sense of salvation history, and start to understand their call to be a part of that history. Suggest Advent as a time to read Hebrew Scriptures, saving Lent for the stories of Jesus. Encourage parents to teach their children to bless themselves on the forehead, lips, and heart before each reading. Publish the readings for the upcoming Sunday in the parish bulletin so that families can become familiar with Scripture.

Finally, parents can bring Scripture and prayer into their family's daily life by introducing a simplified version of the centuries-old prayer called *Lectio Divina* (see sidebar below).

Eucharist as Sacrifice

God calls us in the Liturgy of the Word, and we respond by uniting ourselves with Jesus in the Liturgy of the Eucharist, offering ourselves and our lives with his life. During the preparation of the altar, the presider asks us to pray that our sacrifice be acceptable to the Lord. We know that the Mass is the very real celebration of Jesus' sacrifice on the cross. As we offer this great sacrifice we add our own sacrifices and find meaning and purpose for them through the ritual.

Parents know about sacrifice: giving up sleep to comfort a restless child, wearing retread sneakers so a teen can have new soccer shoes. Parents constantly sacrifice their own needs for the needs of their children. But they are doing their children a disservice if they do not also teach them how to sacrifice. Sacrifice means letting go of being first. It means accepting freely that we will not get everything we want. When children give up something, they learn the discipline of saying no to themselves and choosing a greater good.

God doesn't need our sacrifices, but we do. I remember meeting with a group of teenagers after a twenty-four hour fast from all food. One of the young girls told us that the day of the fast had been her birthday. She described how good she felt about herself. She said she knew that if she could say no to a piece of chocolate fudge cake on her birthday, she would probably be capable of saying no to some of life's bigger temptations.

Sacrifices are not always self-chosen. Parents who sacrifice their sleep for a newborn will tell you they have no choice. Make sure parents and youngsters understand that we do not have to like doing something for it to be considered a sacri-

---

LECTIO DIVINA
Four Traditional Steps

Lectio (reading): the scripture text itself is heard by the reader.

Meditatio (meditation): Go to the story (who would you be, what would you do), or bring the story to you (when have you experienced the elements, emotions, events).

Contemplatio (contemplation): Silent waiting and listening, often done through centering prayer focusing on a word or phrase from the reading.

Oratio (prayer): Whatever prayer or action you are led to (in thanksgiving, petition, contrition, or praise).

---

fice. If a parent can give up sleep night after night without resorting to constant grumbling, or if a youngster can endure a toothache without making everyone else suffer, he or she has certainly made a great sacrifice.

Encourage parents to teach their children how to sacrifice by doing so with them. Suggest they decide as a family what to give up (for example, snacks, television, or soda). Ask them to also show their children how to sacrifice their time and energy by helping a neighbor with yard work without accepting payment, or setting the table when it is someone else's day to do so.

Tell parents to teach their children the response, "May the Lord receive this sacrifice...." Then suggest that on Saturday night or Sunday morning they talk with their children about the sacrifices made that week. Suggest they carry those sacrifices in their hearts to church and give them to God when they say the response during Mass.

Eucharist as Meal

We respond to God's call of love by sharing a meal in communion with those gathered. We recognize and honor God's presence under the appearance of the host and wine and in those who are assembled. The Eucharist is a remembrance of Christ's last meal with his disciples. Today's ritual still has all the rudiments of a special meal: the gathering of people; the telling and retelling of stories; the setting of the table, the blessing of the food before it is eaten, and finally the leave taking. Special meals require a certain air of hospitality and an ambience of style. They are lingered over and appreciated not only for the food served, but for the company gathered.

Unfortunately, today even special meals like Christmas and Thanksgiving are sometimes eaten in front of the television set. The table-fellowship of years ago is almost a lost art for today's children. I remember reading a statistic a few years ago that said the average American family eats only two meals a week together with everyone present. As I watch the young families in my own parish, I wonder how they manage that many. Not only are parents working longer hours, but children are involved in a profusion of extracurricular activities.

Due to the splintering of time and the collision of interests in the average American's life (both young and old), being family is no longer an automatic occurrence. Too often we find households of youngsters and adults who share a roof and finances, but hardly a meal or conversation. In today's American culture becoming a family often takes deliberate, intentional planning.

Catechetical leaders would be wise to remind parents of this reality whenever possible. Point out the need for parents to make family a top priority and to prove their appreciation of the value of family by investing one of their most precious commodities, time. Invite parents to sit down with their calendar to schedule some quality time with their families.

Suggest families begin by taking time for at least one special dinner a week. The food does not need to be fancy, but suggest laying down some ground rules. Tell them to make sure everyone has at least a half-hour set aside for the meal. Take turns saying grace, and limit talk to pleasant subjects. This is no time to ask if homework is done or if permission can be given to stay out late Friday night. Talk should center on the good things that are happening in their lives. The meal should end with prayer (no one leaves early), and clean up should be shared.

When children reach catechetical age they will learn that Eucharist is a meal. Consider the implications if their primary experience of shared food is from a take-out window. If, however, they have experienced, on a regular basis, a sit-down meal that is pleasant and life-giving, perhaps their experience of Eucharist will be the same.

The Real Presence of Christ

This great mystery, "the whole Christ truly, really, and substantially contained" (CCC #1374) in the Eucharist was declared doctrine at the Council of Trent (1551), and remains to this day one of the central beliefs of our faith.

The more we come to know Christ by reading Scripture and engaging in personal and communal prayer, the more we will enter into the mystery of Christ's Real Presence in the Eucharist. The more we come to know Christ as Eucharist, the more we come to know ourselves as Eucharist. It all begins with learning about Jesus.

Remind parents that if children do not hear them talk about God and Jesus as realities in their lives, it will be difficult for God and Jesus to become real for the children. Suggest parents end family prayer with the words, "through Christ the Lord," or "in Jesus' name." Introduce parents to meditation and centering prayer, the prayer of quiet. Ask them to share these age-old prayer forms with their children. Suggest parents drop into church occasionally and sit quietly in front of the tabernacle. Remind them that two or three minutes for small children is long enough for quiet prayer.

The Liturgical Year

For years I had in my office a poster depicting the Liturgical Year as a circle of greens and reds and purples. This image of a circle changed for me when I read a *Youth Update* written by Sr. Sandra DeGidio, OSM (*St. Anthony Messenger Press*, December 1999). Sr. DeGidio wrote that while the Liturgical Year may repeat itself over and over, the movement is not circular; it is an upward spiral. As the liturgical seasons change, we change. Year after year we are invited to grow in our understanding and participation in the liturgy.

Each year we are encouraged to listen to Scripture as it unwinds the story of God's self-revelation and reveals the truth about who we are and who we are called to be. We are invited to hear the readings as if they were new and different because each year finds us new and different from the year before.

The church year is made up of two great cycles, Incarnation and Resurrection, and the ordinary time that separates them. The two cycles celebrating Christmas and Easter are each preceded by a period of preparation and anticipation and followed by a season of celebration. The ordinary days of Summer and Winter are a celebration of Sundays, reminding us of the new life that is ours through Christ's Resurrection, and challenging us to follow Christ in our everyday lives. Each season has its own rhythm and mood, its own symbols and rites.

Bringing the Liturgical Seasons Home

One way of celebrating the church year at home is for families to set up their own home altar. It can be a small, separate table in a corner, or on top of a mantel or bookshelf. The family needs just three tablecloths: green, purple, and white. A strip of cloth or a length of ribbon can be added on appropriate days: red for Pentecost and Palm Sunday; blue for Marian holidays. The crucifix, Bible, and special family keepsakes can be placed on top. Before the home altar families can gather for morning or night prayer, as well as on other occasions.

I suggest families use their own kitchen or dining room table as their home altar. This is where they share their life stories as well as their meals. Three small table runners, or 6x6 inch squares of cloth (green, purple, and white), can serve as the base for a candle centerpiece. Each family can make their own paschal candle, decorating it with the traditional symbols (the alpha and omega, a cross and the current year), or a family can decide on its own symbols. Some people's tables inevitably collect the day's clutter, and that is fine. In many ways that clutter tells the family stories and represents the crosses as well as the keepsakes. All are appropriate for a home altar.

During Advent and Lent use a wreath in the center of the table. Advent wreaths can be made with fresh evergreens every year or made and saved from year to year with artificial evergreens. Lenten wreaths can be as simple as a hand-colored paper plate with six votive candles, or a crown of thorns encircling one large candle.

There is no problem coming up with ideas for seasonal at-home activities. The problem is getting these ideas into parents' hands and convincing them to use them.

I found three excellent liturgical year resources that meet my personal criteria for effective family faith formation. *Generations of Faith* , *Kitchen Table Gospel*, and *People of Faith: Generations Learning Together*. These resources offer ideas for parents and children to share their faith with each other as they celebrate the liturgical seasons at home. All three include suggestions for parish-based intergenerational gatherings to bring families together with other parishioners to build community and offer support.

Whether you use these resources or others for intergenerational learning, you will have to tailor the package to meet the specific needs of your parish. Also, be sure to evaluate the process afterwards. Save resources and record ideas so they can be shared with other catechetical leaders and possibly reworked for other gatherings.

CROWN OF THORNS LENTEN WREATH

The wreath can be made from any thorny bush. Fresh cut branches easily bend into a crown of thorns. Tie ends together with thin purple ribbon. Make sure to use thick work gloves when handling the branches.

When my children were young we put jellybeans in the center of the wreath. After dinner each child could take a jellybean for every good deed, extra prayer, or special "goody" done without that day. When they were old enough to read, the ritual changed. On Ash Wednesday we each received six rectangles of purple or pink paper. We wrote six suggested activities: two good deeds, two special prayers, and two sacrifices. We folded the rectangles, sealed them with tape, and marked them with a heart for good deeds, a pretzel for prayers, and a cross for sacrifices. After dinner throughout Lent we took turns picking and reading our selections.

The children were free to write anything they wanted, but every year the same good deeds and sacrifices would turn up. Giving up soda, chocolate, or chips were favorite sacrifices. Prayers tended to change year to year depending on family or world needs.

Liturgy of the Hours

Since the first century, Christians have prayed the Liturgy of the Hours. This daily public prayer of the church began with ordinary people, but in time was relegated almost exclusively to the domain of monastics and religious orders. The Hours are closely connected to the Eucharist and are meant to prepare one for the Eucharistic Celebration or keep one connected to the sacramental action throughout the day. Today, some parishes and individuals are reclaiming this ritualized prayer of the church. While the litanies, readings, and prayers may change from day to day, the format for the Liturgy of the Hours stays the same.

Encourage families to say this traditional prayer at home. Suggest they use the same format but keep the prayers and readings simple and brief (the younger the family, the shorter the service). Ask parents or older children to choose only a sentence or two from the psalms and from the gospel of the day. Suggest they celebrate their daily ritual in the same place each time, such as in front of the home altar, around the kitchen table, or sitting together in the living room.

Inform parents that they are joining with the larger church, since we know that at every hour of the day the Liturgy of the Hours is being said at some place in the world. Help them understand that their prayer is connected to this universal prayer. Ask them to help their children also make this connection.

LITURGY OF THE HOURS SIMPLIFIED

The liturgy is prayed in two parts, so divide your family into two groups with at least one reader in each group. Eventually the responses can be memorized. Bow heads when the Father, Son, and Holy Spirit are mentioned.

Sign of the Cross (all)

[Stand] God, come to my assistance.

    Lord, make haste to help me.

    Glory be to the Father and
      the Son and the Holy Spirit.

    As it was in the beginning,
      is now, and ever shall be.

    Amen.

[Sit] Reading of the psalm

[Sit] Reading of the gospel

[Sit] We give thanks and pray….

[Individuals give thanks and pray for what they need.]

[Stand] May the Lord bless us,
    protect us from evil,
and bring us to
    everlasting life.

    Glory be to the Father…

    As it was in the beginning….

Sacraments

My favorite definition of "sacrament" is also the briefest: visible signs of invisible grace. We believe

God calls each of us into an intimate relationship of love. God's invitation is called grace. If God had a hand, it would always be stretched out to us in love. God's extended hand is like actual grace. When we reach back and grab God's hand and live hand-in-hand with him, that's sanctifying grace. When we answer God's invitation, his call, and live in God's love, we are living in sanctifying grace. In his book *Christ: The Sacrament of the Encounter with God*, E. Schillebeeckx tells us:

> The act itself of this encounter of God and man which on earth can take place only in faith, is what we call salvation. On God's part this encounter involves a disclosure of himself by revelation, and on the part of man it involves devotion to God's service—that is the religion. This encounter itself, seen from man's side, is the reality of what is called sanctifying grace. (pp. 4-5)

The sacraments are personal encounters with God, recognized and celebrated by the church through finite, visible signs. The drenching with water, the host consumed, the oil poured: these are all visible signs of this encounter witnessed by the church assembled. It is important to remember that sacraments are not just celebrations for the individual and the individual's family; they are celebrations for the whole parish family.

Sacramental Preparation

The definitive aim of catechesis is to bring people into intimate communion with Jesus Christ (see *General Directory for Catechesis* #80). Sacramental catechesis, like all catechesis, involves more than learning about Christ. It involves coming to know Christ in a personal, life-altering way. When this happens in a family setting, an individual's relationship with Christ can be supported and nurtured by the people closest to them. Receiving a sacrament for the first time means encountering Christ through the sacrament of church as well as the particular sacrament's rites and symbols. Preparing for the sacrament should certainly involve the family, the child's first and primary church.

Sacramental preparation also helps the family become more involved in the worship-life of the community, and encourages them to celebrate that worship-life at home. All seven sacraments offer an occasion for the individual, the family, and the whole parish to grow in faith and promise.

Infant Baptism

In a large parish in the archdiocese of Chicago, the parents of a still damp, newly baptized infant watch as several parishioners stand and introduce themselves. They are family parish sponsors who pledge themselves during the baptism ritual to support the parents as they raise their baby in the faith of the community. Throughout the toddler and preschool years, these sponsors will keep in touch with the child's family, offering support and encouragement. The parents know that the parish will also offer opportunities for their family and their sponsoring family to get together for fellowship and learning activities.

The congregation at the nine o'clock Mass were already familiar with the new parents. They had met them when they began preparing for baptism, and again for a special blessing when they entered their final month of pregnancy. They would have a chance to congratulate them on the last Sunday of the month when all the babies baptized at the nine o'clock Masses would have a special reception after Mass.

Preparation

Getting ready for the actual rite of baptism is important, but for some parents, baptism preparation may be their first opportunity to talk about their faith as adults. Preparing for the sacrament of baptism is one of the parish's best opportunities to evangelize these young parents. Consider the following suggestions:

- Take time for parents to look at their own faith and to understand why they want their child to be baptized.
- Discuss with parents their image of God and help them understand that God loves them unconditionally and is eager to be a part of their lives.
- Talk about Jesus Christ as savior and brother.
- Help parents see the parish (the church) as the body of Christ that will always be there to support and challenge them.

Priming parents to be lifelong witnesses of faith to their children is also an important part of baptismal preparation. New parents should understand that because of changes in today's culture, we can no longer assume that children baptized in the faith, and even educated in the faith, will grow up to live or value that faith. We know, however, that the odds are considerably better when children grow up in a home where those values are lived and the faith is articulated.

- Challenge parents to talk to their children about their faith. Recognize the fact that it might be uncomfortable to talk about their faith with their children if they did not grow up in a family that prayed or shared their faith.

- Encourage parents to talk about their faith with each other. Suggest they list the top five things they want their children to know about God and the Catholic church.
- Brainstorm to identify ways parents can create a Christian environment at home. Ask them what in their home says they are Catholic.
- Discuss rituals and their importance in family life and in the life of a Catholic. Share ideas of various rituals they can begin to incorporate in their household.
- Ask parents to put together a plan on how they will share their faith with their children (i.e. prayer time, Sunday Mass, Christian books).
- Discuss their plans at one of your meetings.
- Make copies of their plans. In three years, mail the copy back to them with a letter of encouragement from the parish.

Celebrating Infant Baptism in the Parish
- Introduce parents to the congregation before the baby is born.
- Celebrate baptisms at regular Sunday Liturgies whenever possible.
- When baptism is celebrated outside of Mass, introduce parents and infant the next week at the Mass they regularly attend.
- Have a reception after Mass once a month or four times a year for the newly baptized and their families.
- Ask parishioners to sew the white cloths for baptism, make the candles, or decorate keepsake boxes.
- Invite parents of newly baptized babies to bring their youngster to a religious education class that is learning about baptism to share pictures and talk about their experience of the sacrament.

Celebrating Infant Baptism at Home
- Suggest parents keep the baptismal candle in a safe place and take it out every year on the anniversary of their child's baptism. Tell them to begin a ritual of looking back on the day, recalling the rite, remembering who was there and how they celebrated afterward.
- Send home some holy water with a simple ritual to bless each other and their children.
- Make a keepsake program of the baptismal rite. Leave spaces for the name of the presider and the godparents, titles of songs that were sung, and names of guests who were present.

- Present a small decorated box in which the child's baptismal mementos (candle, white cloth, program, cards) may be kept.

Baptizing Children of Catechetical Age

There are two essential factors to remember when inviting school-aged children to become members of our church. First, the process must always be relevant to the ages of the children (*Rite of Christian Initiation of Adults* #307). Second, the children's parents, as well as their already baptized peers, should be involved in the process (RCIA #308).

Seven-year-olds and twelve-year-olds hear a different beat, see a different world, and speak a different language. As educators we know the difficulty of working with children of such diverse ages in the same learning group. As educators in the faith we fight the temptation to tutor them individually, because doing so would deny the community's role in the process. Many parishes find a solution by offering an intergenerational RCIA process for children. An intergenerational approach offers room for individual attention in a community setting. It also allows both baptized peers and parents to be a part of the process.

If you already have an intergenerational program in your parish that meets on a regular basis (at least monthly), incorporate the new families into this program. Make sure you offer additional gatherings to provide the extra learning and experience the children will need. Adult family members asking for baptism should also be a part of the regular parish RCIA process.

If you do not have an intergenerational program meeting regularly at your parish, consider starting one. Begin by developing a core team of parish adults and established families. When you know the number of families with children seeking baptism, find a sponsor family for each of them. It is an added advantage if the sponsor family has children of the same age.

One resource parishes have found effective is the *God Is Calling* intergenerational catechetical series (St. Anthony Messenger Press, americancatholic.org) which offers a format and materials for integrating the whole family into the children's catechumenate process.

First Eucharist

At St. Francis Parish, with its approximately 12,000 households, the seventy-plus second graders receive First Communion during a regular Sunday Liturgy. They celebrate in small groups of ten to fifteen. A whole pew is saved for their family at the front of church. There is room for parents, siblings, grandparents, and cousins. The pews are marked by colorful banners that were made by the families at a full-day family retreat.

The congregation has met these youngsters and their families twice before. They blessed the children and their parents at the beginning of October when they were enrolled in the preparation process. The children were also introduced at Mass on the first Sunday of the anniversary month of their baptism.

After the Liturgy, there was a special reception for the families, hosted by the previous year's First Communion families. Before they left, the families were reminded to come early to Liturgy on Corpus Christi Sunday (second graders in their First Communion outfits) so they could lead the procession of the Blessed Sacrament.

Preparation

Like baptism, preparation for First Eucharist is an excellent opportunity for evangelization. At a recent national catechetical conference I heard parish ministers vehemently complain about parents who never go to Mass themselves but bring their children for First Communion. When I was a director of religious education in a large suburban parish I had the same complaint. As we talked, we decided that rather than grumble about the situation we would try to see it as a teachable moment. Specifically, we decided to use the time spent in preparing for the sacrament as an opportunity to help the whole family grow in their faith and come closer to the church. Here are some ways to do this:

- Help parents understand their role in the faith development of their children. Make sure they understand that if they want their children to have faith, their children have to see them live out their faith and hear them talk about their faith.
- Offer resources to help parents share their faith at home.
- Discuss the importance of family rituals; offer examples of everyday rituals (dinner prayer) and seasonal rituals (Advent wreath).
- Suggest ways of creating a Christian environment in their home (icons, crucifixes, Bibles, Christian DVDs, books, and so on).

Finally, preparing for First Eucharist is an ideal time to consider family catechesis. When choosing resources remember two essential elements. First, make sure the material provides time for parents to share their faith with their child. (Parents using a textbook to teach their child is not family catechesis: it is homeschooling.) Second, provide periodic parish-based family gatherings for support and fellowship, and to allow parents to ask questions.

Celebrating at the Parish

- In early October have a simple Rite of Enrollment during Mass. Invite families to stand and be blessed. Have children come forward with their names written on a self-sticking tag. Helpers take the tag and place it on a decorated poster.
- Hang the enrollment poster and pictures of the first communicants with a "We welcome you to the table of the Lord" sign in a prominent space.
- Celebrate First Communion in small groups at regular Sunday Liturgies. Keep the numbers low and cut the time of the homily so that Mass does not run too long.
- Have a reception after Mass. Encourage parishioners to congratulate youngsters and their families.
- Ask children in other grades to make "Congratulations" or "God Bless You" cards during religious education class. Present the cards to the communicants after Mass with a keepsake card from the parish.

Celebrating in the Home

- Encourage table fellowship at home—sitting down together to share a meal and enjoy each other's company.
- Provide table prayer cards and wreaths for the liturgical seasons to encourage family prayer at meals.
- Provide a simple recipe for unleavened bread, and ask first communicant families to bake several loaves to be given to other parish families after Thanksgiving day Mass. Have the first communicants hand out the bread along with a short blessing to be said when a parent or grandparent breaks the bread and shares it around the table.
- Have families make a special table runner that reminds them of all the things Eucharist is about.
- Provide resources to help families share the gospel readings each week.

Confirmation

In a small African-American church on the west side of Dayton, Ohio, confirmation was a parish celebration that involved the whole family. Young people ages thirteen to sixteen were invited to receive the sacrament.

Since confirmation is a sacrament of initiation, it was decided that the candidates should be formally presented to the community. At a Sunday

Liturgy, the parent or guardian came to the front of the church and presented the teenager to the parish. Both faced the congregation as the adult announced,

> This is my son/daughter/grandchild, [name], who was baptized in the faith of the community as a baby/child. He/she is ready to begin preparing for confirmation. He/she is a gift to our family, a gift to our parish, and a gift to the world.

At this point the youngster faced the adult (with back to the community to save embarrassment), and the parent/guardian told the young person all the things that made him or her special. A young adult from the parish stepped forward to let the teen know that he or she would be supported. Or as one young man said to his younger protégé, "I've got your back."

For six weeks the candidates met with the young adults and the elders of the parish (one elder for every two or three youngsters). Along with learning about God, church, and confirmation, the adults and teens shared stories, and discussed the music they liked, the heroes they admired, and the possessions they considered most precious.

Confirmation preparation for this parish was designed to incorporate and honor two African-American traditions: the rite of passage and the importance of elders to the community. While confirmation is not a rite of maturity (the traditional rite of passage for African youth), as a sacrament of initiation, it is certainly a rite of passage. Like the rite of enrollment in the RCIA, this simple rite was meant to affirm the young people and let them know they have the support of their community.

Preparation

The parish mentioned above recognized the fact that while at-home family catechesis is always important, adolescents, at this point in their development, often need other adult figures in their lives to listen and look up to. This makes confirmation preparation an ideal time for intergenerational learning. Young people can meet with their peers, their parents, or other adults from the parish in various settings for a variety of learning activities.

Celebrating at the Parish

- Bring the families and young people preparing for First Communion and confirmation together. Let children and adolescents work together making a memento (a candle or scrapbook) for their special occasion while parents learn more about the church into which their children are being further initiated.

- Post the names of the families who are preparing youngsters for confirmation. Ask parishioners to adopt a family and pray for them by name. If space permits, invite these people to the confirmation celebration. At the reception afterward, encourage families and prayer partners to get together.
- Offer various service opportunities for the family at the parish such as working on the parish garden or stuffing bulletins.
- Whenever possible use the phrase "service activity" rather than "service project." A project has a beginning and an end. Service is the lifelong vocation of the Christian.
- Recognize the families during the confirmation service. Affirm and thank them for their efforts in bringing their children up in the faith.
- Ask various parish commissions how they can incorporate the newly confirmed in their ministries. Put together a list for confirmandi with an explanation of what the ministries are about.

Celebration at Home
- Ask candidates to look through any pictures they might have of their baptism. Have them interview their parents about what they remember about the day.
- Send home the list of parish ministries available for young people to become more involved at the parish. Invite parents to go over the list with their child and help him or her discern where his or her gifts can best be used.
- Suggest a service activity in which the whole family can be involved. When possible coordinate activities so that more than one family can work together.
- If they are not already doing so, encourage parents to bless their children (with or without holy water) on special occasions, for example, the first day of school, before a test, when leaving for vacation.

First Reconciliation

Assumption parishioners were used to intergenerational gatherings. We had been involved in Generations of Faith for years. Six times a year we gathered folks of all ages to learn and celebrate together. This particular year our topic had been healing and reconciliation.

During the gathering time I gave a brief talk on the sacrament of reconciliation. I offered the same description of sacraments given early in this chapter: God reaching for us and our reaching back. I used my hands to exemplify this point with fingers intertwined to illustrate sanctifying grace. I explained that venial sin (gossiping, not listening to parents, and so on) is like loosening our grip with God's hand. Mortal sin is deliberately rejecting God and is like letting go all together. I used my hand to demonstrate, turning the back of my hand to the palm of God's. Finally, I clasped both hands tightly together and explained that the sacrament of reconciliation is our choosing to turn back to God, once again secure in his gentle grasp.

At the reconciliation service that ended our gathering, four priests stood in the front of church giving absolution. As I watched the parishioners in line, I swallowed hard when I saw one of our first graders receive absolution from one of the visiting priests. At the party afterward, I went up to the priest and told him he had given first reconciliation to a six-year-old who had had no formal sacramental preparation. He asked me which child it was. Obviously, that brief explanation of the sacrament had been simple enough for a first grader to understand.

Preparation

Jesus Christ, our brother and redeemer, was the great reconciler. He spent his life trying to restore peace and harmony to the world and into the lives of all those he encountered. As his disciples we are commissioned to do the same. We begin our efforts with ourselves, realizing that it is impossible to give to others what we ourselves do not possess. The sacrament that celebrates our efforts to restore peace and make things right in our own life is called "penance," or reconciliation.

Parents of children receiving first reconciliation are often invited to receive the sacrament with their children. A priest friend once commented that many of these parents are reluctantly celebrating their *second* reconciliation as their children celebrate their first. It is admittedly difficult to tell our sins to another person, and Catholics as well as non-Catholics often wonder why we can't just tell God we are sorry without having to go through the middleman. Helping parents prepare their children provides an opportunity to answer that question.

- Ask parents about their own personal experience of the sacrament. Ask non-Catholic parents to talk about their impression of confession from movies or television.

- Admit that fear and hesitation are natural reactions to telling another person about our own shortcomings or sins.
- Offer the historical background of reconciliation as a bridge to a broader, healthier understanding of the sacrament. The church's earliest experiences of penance teach us that when we fail to live up to our Christian commitment, we are failing the community, not just God. The priest is a representative of both God and the community. He gives absolution in the name of both.
- Ask parents to make a conscious effort not to pass on any negative feelings to their children. Explain your hope that as they listen to the history of the sacrament they will readjust their attitude toward it.

Celebrating at the Parish
- Plan the reconciliation service at a time when the whole family can attend.
- Make sure to invite enough priests so that everyone can receive the sacrament within a reasonable amount of time.
- At the regular lenten parish penitential service introduce the families with children who have received first reconciliation.
- Host a party afterwards. Even if the sacrament is celebrated in Lent, it is a special occasion. Offer cookies and punch or pizza and soda. Having a party will remind everyone that this sacrament, like all sacraments, is a joyful event, a celebration.

Celebrating at Home
- Give parents a simple penance service for families to pray at home.
- Prepare home materials to assist parents in helping their children develop a healthy conscience.
- Ask parents to help their youngsters write their own "Sorry Prayer." Make sure it is simple and includes the three important parts of an Act of Contrition: saying they are sorry; telling God they will do their best not to commit the same offense again; and asking for God's help.
- Suggest that parents and children help each other develop an examination of conscience relevant to their age and lifestyle.

The Remaining Three Sacraments

The other three sacraments—anointing of the sick, matrimony, and holy orders—are often overlooked by parishes as opportunities for family faith formation. Yet when we consider the effect of change on family dynamics, it would seem facing serious illness, getting married, or celebrating holy orders would certainly constitute life-changing events.

Unfortunately, catechetical leaders are already overburdened just accomplishing the present tasks on their job description. The idea of taking on more sacraments, indeed taking on any of the ideas in this chapter, might seem daunting. If, however, you approach faith formation as the *General Directory for Catechesis* suggests, the responsibility for faith formation becomes the responsibility of the whole parish. Other ministries, such as worship or outreach, can be encouraged to help involve families in the preparation for the sacraments. Below is one simple suggestion for each of the three remaining sacraments.

Anointing of the Sick. Parishes can celebrate a communal anointing service during or after a Sunday Liturgy. Send home some holy water and a simple prayer blessing that a parent can say while blessing a sick child or spouse.

Matrimony. Suggest that the immediate family gather before the wedding and pray together. Encourage parents and siblings to ask for God's blessing and God's healing spirit to free the bride or groom from any childhood or young adult hurts that were inflicted, consciously or unconsciously, by other family members.

Holy Orders. Ask families to talk about the different ministries in the church as they pray for the vocations to fill them. Suggest they discuss their own gifts and pray for each other, their own work, and the parish ministries in which they are involved.

Conclusion

As church, we celebrate God with us in the Eucharist as we read Scripture, raise the host and cup, and watch the young and old return from communion. We celebrate God with us, season after liturgical season, through the familiar rhythm and consistent pattern of salvation history, using color and texture, music and readings to set a tone and establish an atmosphere. We celebrate God with us using concrete signs as our touchstones, signs that hold within them God's constant and open-ended invitation to life, elements like water and oil, bread and wine.

As a family, we celebrate God with us when we gather around our own kitchen tables, give thanks, and break bread. We celebrate God with us in all the seasons of our family's life by linking the stories of salvation to our own stories of birth, death, and resurrection. We celebrate God with us in concrete signs like hugs and extra cookies, Band-aids® and handing over the car keys. Each day we discover new visible and concrete signs to express our love for each other, a love that mirrors God's love for us, a for-better-or-worse love that will last forever. As family, we were called by God to live in God and love with God. Families answer God's call every day as they pray, play, learn, reconcile, and serve together. They answer God's call as individuals and as the most intimate community of church.

Reflection Questions

1. What is the connection between how a parish prays and how a family prays?
2. How does your parish support, nurture, and provide resources for the worship life of the home church?
3. What impact is possible if a parish were to prepare the household or family for a sacrament instead of just preparing the individual?

References

Catechism of the Catholic Church. Washington, DC: United States Catholic Conference, 1997.

Flannery, Austin, O.P., general editor. *Decree on the Apostolate of the Laity*. Document of Vatican II. Northport, NY: Costello Publishing Company, 1996.

Richstatter, Thomas, O.F.M. *The Sacraments: How Catholics Pray*. Cincinnati: St. Anthony Messenger Press, 1995.

Schillebeeckx, E. *Christ the Sacrament of the Encounter with God*. Franklin, WI: Sheed and Ward, 1999.

Chapter Nine

Supporting Families in Serving Others

Eugene C. Roehlkepartain
& Jenny Friedman

Editor's Note

Discipleship challenges all Christians to reach beyond themselves in works of mercy and works of justice for others. As families grow in faith, they are challenged to look beyond their own struggles and engage in service for others. Gene Roehlkepartain and Jenny Friedman bring outstanding expertise and years of experience in helping parishes and congregations develop a vision and practice for family outreach and service. Jenny and Gene know two secrets: 1) serving others is central to shaping one's faith identity, and 2) as families engage in justice and service they grow in love for each other and can often heal their own wounds. You will appreciate that the concepts presented in this chapter are rooted in sound research.

Eugene C. Roehlkepartain is senior advisor, office of the president, for Search Institute, Minneapolis, Minnesota, a nonprofit organization dedicated to promoting healthy children, youth, and communities (www.search-institute.org). He leads the institute's efforts to address faith communities, families, and spiritual development. He is author or co-author of several books, including Growing Up Generous: Engaging Youth in Giving and Serving *(Alban Institute),* An Asset Builder's Guide to Service-Learning *(Search Institute), and* Building Assets in Congregations *(Search Institute).*

Jenny Friedman, Ph.D., is founder and executive director of Doing Good Together, a nonprofit organization dedicated to encouraging, supporting, and educating parents and caregivers who want to engage with their children in volunteering, charitable giving, and social, environmental, and political action (www.doinggoodtogether.org). She is author of The Busy Family's Guide to Volunteering *(Robins Lane Press).*

One of the most important tasks for the church today is to promote the faith growth of families by encouraging families to share, celebrate, and live their faith at home and in the world" (*Renewing the Vision*, p. 12).

Serving others, addressing injustice, and meeting human needs are central to Catholic teachings and, indeed, the teachings of all major religious traditions. John E. Tropman writes that "the central features of the Catholic ethic include orientations toward the community, toward family, toward the self-in-context....There is a tradition of 'share-ity' and a bias in favor of the poor" (p. 271). Similarly, the U.S. Conference of Catholic bishops has stated that "Our faith is profoundly social....We cannot be called truly 'Catholic' unless we hear and heed the church's call to serve those in need and work for justice and peace. We cannot call ourselves followers of Jesus unless we take up his mission of bringing 'good news to the poor, liberty to captives, and new sight to the blind'" (*Communities of Salt and Light*, p. 3).

Given the central role of family in shaping a person's faith identity and commitments throughout the life cycle, how does serving others become integral to family life? And how do parishes nurture and support this commitment? One might hope that it comes naturally, something that every family just does. Yet surveys of the general public suggest that most families do not see serving others as an integral part of family life. Consider these examples:

Independent Sector found that, in 1998, only twenty-eight percent of American adults reported volunteering with other family members (*America's Family Volunteers*).

Another poll in 1997 found that thirty-four percent of respondents had volunteered with their spouses in the past year, and twenty-four percent said they had volunteered with their children (Lutheran Brotherhood Reports).

Slightly higher levels of family service are evident among religious families. A Search Institute study of five Protestant denominations found that thirty-six percent of young people said their families sometimes or often do family projects to help other people (*Effective Christian Education*).

Only about half of young people (forty-eight percent) surveyed in public schools said that their parents spend a lot of time helping others. Another third (thirty-five percent) were not sure ("Engaging Families in Service").

A pilot study of 1,500 youth and adults in fifteen U.S. congregations found that twenty-seven percent of respondents said their family helps other people together (*Building Assets, Strengthening Faith*).

Although serving others is an integral part of faith, relatively few families make serving others an ongoing part of life together. If individuals volunteer or serve, it is generally disconnected from the family. In many congregations, service and justice activities are age-segregated, with adults and children involved in separate projects. This reality represents a major loss of opportunity for family ministry and parish life.

Focusing on *family* service can be powerful for a congregation, helping parishioners discover not only what gifts each individual has to offer others, but how the family, together, will live out its sense of purpose in the community and world. In this chapter, we review the opportunities and challenges for parishes to support families in serving others. Then we highlight strategies and best practices for creating a continuum of opportunities that can help make service to others an integral part of family and parish life.

Why Bother Engaging Families in Serving Others?

Engaging with their families in service can be a valuable opportunity for parents to pass on key values to their children, for family members to discuss important social issues with one another, and for parishioners to make a real difference in the community while spending time with loved ones. Indeed, offering opportunities for family service has multiple benefits for strengthening families, building communities, nurturing faith and compassion in children, and strengthening congregations.

Strengthening Family Bonds

Today's families are scattered and busy, making many families hesitate to commit time to "one more thing." But a hurry-up life is one of the best reasons for families to volunteer together. Family service allows families to live out their Christian calling to serve others while also giving them an oasis of meaningful time together to express shared values, inspiring important conversations that draw families closer. It increases children's appreciation and respect for their parents as they see them caring for their community (Littlepage, *Family Volunteering*). Once established, volunteering together can become a long-standing family tradition.

A number of years ago, writer Dolores Curran asked 555 professionals who work with families what traits they most often found in healthy families. Among the top fifteen traits in her study was "valuing service," which she described as "families looking beyond themselves and their own individual lives" (*Traits of a Healthy Family*, p. 245). Barbara Carlson, the director of the Minnesota-based family advocacy organization, Putting Family First, is even more adamant. She has told me that family volunteer work is one of the three most important ways to keep families strong.

Nurturing Faith and Values

Adults engaging with their children or grandchildren in serving others provides children a powerful opportunity to deepen their faith. "My children learned more volunteering than I could teach in ten years of Sunday school," said Karen Leavitt, a parent of three children who spent several weeks one summer aiding victims of a fire near their Durango, Colorado, home. In fact, research finds that family service is more significant in faith formation than Bible study, Sunday school, or participation in worship (*Effective Christian Education*).

Family service also can provide a powerful antidote to our culture's incessant messages of competition, self-absorption, and materialism. Volunteering is a hands-on way to teach children the values of kindness, compassion, tolerance, community responsibility, and good citizenship. Family service may also provide one of the few opportunities young people have to interact with people of other backgrounds, breaking down stereotypes of age, class, and race. Children can better put their own problems in perspective when they see what others struggle with, enhancing both empathy and gratitude (Littlepage, *Family Volunteering*). "It sounds clichéd, but my kids realize that small things they do can make a big difference," says Tara Whalen, of Norwalk, Connecticut, who's volunteered at AmeriCares with her family since her oldest child, now eleven, was a baby. "My four kids have become much more appreciative of what they have because they realize there are others who aren't as fortunate as they are."

Finally, family volunteerism cultivates a lifelong commitment to service and justice. Adults who began volunteering as youth are twice as likely to volunteer as those who did not, and those who volunteered as youth and whose parents volunteered gave their time most generously as adults (*Engaging Youth in Lifelong Service*). When individuals learn the value of service at an early age, they are likely to continue contributing to the community throughout their lives.

Kathleen and James McGinnis write that "our commitment to parenting can be precisely one of the basic ways in which we can answer the call to justice and peace. Rather than experiencing frustration at how little time is 'left over' for social concerns, we discover that parenting abounds with ways to integrate social concerns into daily life" (*Parenting for Peace and Justice*, p. 144). They explain: "We want our children to experience social action as a regular part of family life....If social action is experienced by children as a 'special extra,' tacked on if there is time, then it may well remain that way for them as adults" (pp. 95-96).

Strengthening Congregations

Family service can promote loyalty and commitment to the congregation among young people and adults. Evidence suggests that as children grow, they spend increasingly less time in activities related to a religious institution. But youth who are involved in community service through their congregation are more likely to say their parish matters to them and to report that they plan to stay involved in the church as adults (*The Teaching Church*). And when families serve together, it follows that the entire family—both young people and adults—will be more invested in the church.

Family service can also create increased community exposure and visibility for the parish. Because family service is unique, worthwhile, and innovative, it's an opportunity to attract community attention to the congregation's outreach efforts (Hegel, *Family Volunteering*).

Benefiting Communities

Family service can bring new energy to traditional volunteer opportunities. When Jenny and her preschool children delivered meals to the homebound, they were much more effective in bringing joy and companionship to the people they served than if she went alone. (The elderly people were thrilled to be handed their meal by a grinning three-year-old.) These types of early volunteer jobs can inspire young people to continue making a positive difference as adults, creating a new generation of volunteers and philanthropists.

Finally, family service also increases charitable contributions. Surveys indicate that family volunteers gave a greater portion of their income to charity than non-family volunteers (*America's Family Volunteers*). If your parish has specific activities that need funding, it's possible that unexpected largess could come your way as a result of the giving spirit you instill.

Challenges in Launching a Family Service Emphasis

Despite its tremendous potential, family service is rarely considered a core part of family ministry and parish faith formation. Why aren't more parishes seeking to engage families in service? Why aren't most families themselves engaging in service together? Several factors are often at work.

Narrow Understanding of "Family"

When some people hear the term "family service" or "family volunteering," they presume that it's an opportunity for only certain types of families. In reality, family service is most compelling when it engages people of all ages and in many different circumstances in serving others alongside those who are most important to them. Thus, it may include parents with children and teenagers, young adults, empty-nest adults, retirees, couples, grandparents with grandchildren, aunts and uncles with nieces and nephews, foster families…the list goes on and on.

Families that have it together can serve others together, and so can families that are struggling, as service can help them see themselves in a new light, not just as needy, but also needed. We encourage everyone to participate in "family service" with whomever they consider "family."

Age-Segregated Programming

Family members have served others together throughout recorded history in both formal and informal ways. Yet as churches and other organizations have adopted formal programs and created more age-specific service and volunteer programming, families have had fewer opportunities to serve together. For example, some service activities limit participation to older youths (e.g., ages 16-plus) for legal and liability reasons. Or there is simply a perception that there are no activities that generations can enjoy doing together. The result is that many families either serve others on their own or split up to participate in age-specific activities.

Stretched and Stressed Families

One of the potential challenges in engaging families in serving others is the stress already placed on many families. Would this focus only add to the demands on families? While he agrees that many families may not naturally gravitate to service, Leif Kehrwald suggests that serving others can have a healing, renewing effect on families. "Faced with so many problems of their own," he writes, "many families are not motivated to serve others. Yet often, acts of selfless mercy can transform woes into healing as well as bring help to those in greater need" ("Family and Christian Practice," p. 56).

Adding to this perspective, sociologist Penny Edgell Becker's study of the "time bind" and congregations found that "what church members find most compelling, what causes them to make the time for church in the context of a busy life, is the sense that they get something there that they get nowhere else, something worth making a commitment to" (p. 25). Family service can be just that kind of opportunity.

Emphasis on Families as "Consumers" of Ministry

Too often, families are viewed primarily as "consumers" of congregational life. Leaders seek to understand and meet family needs and to make sure families are satisfied. Those emphases certainly play a role, but they can also undermine an understanding of families as contributors to the congregation's mission and ministries. That contribution is not limited to their participation in activities, but through the way they live out their faith in daily family life. Paradoxically, recognition of families as contributors to—not just recipients of—the congregation's ministries will likely meet deeper family needs than would be met through simply trying to "serve" families by "delivering" family-friendly programs.

Inadequate Attention to Effective Practices

Many service experiences for youth, families, adults, or intergenerational groups are poorly planned and implemented. Writing about youth service (but applicable also to family service), Thomas Bright and John Roberto note: "Many service projects are so poorly planned that they do more harm than good to youth and the people they are trying to help....It is hard to believe this is what Jesus had in mind when he spoke of serving the needs of others" (p. 3). People in congregations seem to recognize the gap in family service. An exploratory survey of 1,600 youth and adults in fifteen self-selected U.S. congregations found that only one-third believed their congregation does very or extremely well at providing opportunities for families to serve others together (*Building Assets, Strengthening Faith*).

The good news is that a great deal has been learned in the past thirty years in the fields of service-learning, volunteerism, advocacy, and missions. These practices include active engagement of those performing the service in planning the experience, a partnership with the community being served, and a strong component of reflection on the service experience.

Strategies for Parishes to Engage Families

By offering the basic teaching, support, opportunities, encouragement, and guidance parishes can help congregants serve others as a family. The key to integrating family service into all aspects of congregational life— including education, social ministries, worship, and special events—is to create systems and opportunities that fit their church's character, priorities, and strengths. A real commitment to family service is, of course, not a one-time event, but is cultivated through a web of experiences and relationships across many years. Over time, congregants will begin to view family service as something normative, expected, and celebrated as integral to being part of the community of faith.

Emphasize the Parish-Family Partnership

"We believe that the family is the *domestic church* or the *church of the home* and that the family shares in one and the same mission that Christ gives to the whole church," writes John Roberto. "We believe that effective ministry with families involves building a partnership between the congregation and the home, which focuses on the unique responsibilities that each have in promoting faith growth" (p. 60).

Unfortunately, this theologically sound perspective rarely becomes manifest in the day-to-day life of churches and families. Instead, the emphasis is placed on how families support the church and its programs, rather than on how the parish equips and encourages families to discover and live out their mission and ministry in the world. Ben Freudenburg argues that "we need to empower and equip parents to make good choices for their family's faith development. That means we'll need to teach them about their role, encourage them to embrace it, give them training and resources to do it at home, and then pattern our church's programming and structure to support them in their role" (*The Family-Friendly Church*, p. 113).

Raise Awareness of Family Service

Continuing support and enthusiasm from within the congregation is essential to any family service program, so it is critical to educate parishioners about its benefits, assist them in exploring the link to their values and faith, and celebrate the difference parish families are making in the community. Remind families that whether they work together to deliver meals to the homebound, advocate for social change, foster animals awaiting adoption, write a letter to free a prisoner of conscience, or visit a nursing home, they are acting out their spirituality—together with their family—in a powerful way. Emphasizing the collective power of families serving together will inspire and motivate them to continue to reach out.

Explore the religious roots of serving others with the congregation. You can discuss how works of mercy and works of justice are tied to Catholic traditions, beliefs, and sacred writings. During homilies and at other times, priests can highlight the gospel imperatives for service and the value of families serving together. Parishioners can tell stories about their family volunteer experiences, explaining the impact on their faith and life.

Provide Opportunities for Family Service

Getting started with family service will be easier with the right planning. Following a few basic guidelines for effective family service opportunities will make success more likely:

- Make the activities meaningful, so that every family member, regardless of age, can contribute in a significant way.
- Supply "mentor families" to other families that have had little or no experience in service. These mentor families can provide encouragement and support to families new to service and can help with recruitment, preparation, and reflection.
- Offer various options to suit families with different ages, interests, time constraints, and locations. Reach out to engage a broad range of families, not just those who always "show up." Encourage those families that are already involved to extend personal invitations— family to family—to participate.
- Include preparation and reflection as part of any church-sponsored service activity. This will enable participants to delve more deeply into the experience and find out what it reveals about their values, faith, and beliefs.

Here are some ways to integrate family service activities into congregational life.

Expand current service activities to specifically involve families. Most congregations have limited time and resources. Initially, you may want to determine how families can be integrated into your already existing events, classes, or activities. This may include involving parents in youth service-learning, asking any current partner agencies about opportunities that families can enjoy, making service a part of congregation-wide family events, or expanding mission trips to include families with children.

Make ongoing family volunteer opportunities available. Establish relationships with local agencies to provide ongoing opportunities for family service. Your parish might partner with a local nursing home so that interested families can adopt a grandparent, host a bingo night, or drive residents to doctor's appointments. You might team with a local soup kitchen, homeless shelter, or crisis nursery to provide meals, do repairs, or hold a diaper drive. Your parish can offer families the opportunity to sponsor refugees, pick up trash along a local waterway, or donate items for an annual garage sale to raise money for hunger relief.

Offer some simple "in-house" activities. Although some families are enthusiastic about and ready for community ministry, others may be more comfortable initially with simple service activities they can complete at the church. For example, families can meet to assemble birthday bags to donate to a local food pantry, make "no-sew" fleece blankets for a crisis nursery, or create greeting cards for hospitalized children. Consider personalizing these activities by inviting someone from (or familiar with) the community being served to share the stories, realities, and culture of the community.

Organize regular family service days and events. Invite families to spend Martin Luther King, Jr. Day of Service, National Family Volunteer Day, or Earth Day together engaged in a church-wide service activity. (Visit www.pointsoflight.org/programs/seasons/ for information on year-round national and international service days to which you can link your efforts.) Some congregations have spent this time boxing food for shelters and soup kitchens, working on habitat restoration, or distributing health care information.

No matter which particular activities are chosen, it's important to plan the experience so that volunteers learn and grow from it. That means beginning the day with prayers and a discussion of concerns and expectations. Afterward, gather (perhaps with a shared meal) to talk about the activity, asking participants to tell stories and describe their experience. Discuss how church members might use the service experience to enrich and give meaning to their lives, making the connection to their faith. "A full spiritual life for us and our children," writes author and Christian educator Karen Marie Yust, "combines these elements of reflection and action in a never-ending movement of journeying inward toward God and outward toward neighbors who are both friends and strangers" (*Real Kids, Real Faith*).

Consider organizing a family mission trip. These more intense, long-term service experiences can be life altering. They can enable families to understand poverty through immersion, provide family members with a common vision, purpose, and experience, and present an opportunity to build meaningful, lifelong memories together. One fourteen-year-old who helped build a health clinic in Nueva Vida, Nicaragua with her family and other church members said, "It felt so good to know I was helping out and making a difference in people's lives. It's changed me forever."

Encourage Independent and Family-Initiated Activities

In addition to sponsoring service activities, churches can make families aware of opportunities in their communities and teach them how to design and implement their own volunteer activities. Here's how to encourage and facilitate the process.

Hold a family service fair. Invite local nonprofits to present ideas for family-friendly opportunities in your community. Include both direct service opportunities (e.g., tutoring and serving meals to the homeless) and social justice and advocacy activities (e.g., human rights and environmental projects). Be sure to include options for all types of families to get involved in both big and small ways.

Provide resources for families. Invest in books families can use in your church library and publicize where they are. Some examples include *The Busy Family's Guide to Volunteering, Raising Kids Who Will Make a Difference, Parenting for Peace and Justice, Teaching Your Kids to Care, Family: The Forming Center, The Giving Family,* and *Family Serve: Volunteer Opportunities for Families.* (For a review of family service resources for congregations and families, see *Engaging Families in Service.*)

Also include children's books that focus on caring for others (*The Legend of Bluebonnet* by Tomie de Paola), service to the community (*Uncle Willie and the Soup Kitchen* by Dyanne DiSalvo Ryan), and important social issues (*The Lorax* by Dr. Seuss). These books will help parents initiate conversations with their children about the value of community involvement.

Become a clearinghouse for local opportunities. Even those families that don't normally attend congregation-wide functions may be interested in serving with their own families in ways that meet their particular interests, ages, location, and time constraints. Ask a parishioner to research family-friendly volunteer opportunities in the community and present new ideas in the church bulletin or newsletter each month, or list them on the church Web site. Be certain to include both one-time and ongoing service activities. Give families copies of the reproducible sheet titled "Service: A Family Affair" (see handout at the end of this chapter) to encourage them to come up with their own projects.

Celebrate what families are already doing. Find both formal and informal ways to honor the service that families are providing, whether or not they are sponsored by the church. Highlight any completed family service activities in talks or speeches, write articles on such experiences for the church newsletter, share a letter from a grateful service recipient, encourage media coverage, or throw a family-volunteer recognition party. This kind of recognition can encourage future commitments from families already serving, and can foster a communal spirit of volunteerism that will inspire other families to reach out as well.

Weaving Effective Family Service into Parish Life

It's easy to think of family service as something else you need to do—a new program, a new activity, a new committee—when your schedule is already overflowing. But with some creative planning, family service can become a sustained and sustaining emphasis throughout congregational life. The long-term goal must be that family service become integrated and integral to parish life—a norm and expectation that is broadly supported and reinforced.

We believe that family service fits well with three cornerstones of parish life:

1. service and social action;
2. education and formation;
3. worship.

Religious education or formation focuses on teaching the faith; mission projects focus on faith in action; and worship focuses on celebrating God's presence in people's lives and the world. When woven together through family service, these three priorities enrich each other, the parish, families, and the broader community. To see the connections, we draw on a four-phase framework for service-learning called PARR: Preparation, Action, Reflection, and Recognition (*An Asset Builder's Guide to Service-Learning*).

Preparation: Getting Started on the Right Foot

Careful planning and preparation are essential for designing family service-learning experiences that will have a positive impact on the families and those being served. Preparation for family service can involve the following:

- Get to know the families in your parish. What are they already doing? What are they ready to do? What are they called to do?
- Clarify your goals for the families involved, the community that is being served, and the parish. How are you—and they—hoping to grow through the experience? How can you be instrumental in increasing the chances that growth will occur?
- Prepare people educationally and spiritually for the experience.

Host religious education opportunities that examine the issues behind the problem being addressed. Underscore the spiritual call to serve others during Mass. Invite the whole congregation to support and encourage the families who are involved. Provide background information that can address any misperceptions, and train families in site-specific skills.

- Be clear about who will be involved (both those serving and those being served), then ensure that they are meaningfully engaged from the beginning. Design service opportunities that tap the diverse strengths of all ages of family members who are engaged. An elderly grandparent may not be the right person to hammer shingles on the roof, but she may have excellent organizational skills to ensure that the right people are at the right place doing the right thing at the right time.

- Offer a variety of options and opportunities for families to get involved depending on their schedule, interests, and level of commitment. Identify some opportunities that individual families can do on their own as well as opportunities for several families to serve together.

- Think through the logistics so that the experience goes as smoothly as possible. Simple oversights ("Did anyone remember to bring the tool box?") can quickly undermine positive experiences!

- Even if families are not actively involved in the service-learning activity, keep them informed about what's happening. Encourage them to talk with their children about what they are experiencing and learning.

Action: Making a Difference in the World

The action step is the most visible and tangible part of the service-learning process, and many people immediately gravitate toward the "doing." Here are some suggestions for ensuring that the action phase in family service is effective and connected to the rest of the process.

- Maintain the safety, health, and energy of all family members, keeping in mind that appropriate activities for some family members may be too difficult (or boring) for other family members.

- Know your plans for reflection and recognition in advance of action. This will help everyone be attentive to, document, and remember the service experience. Family members can be assigned to videotape or otherwise document the experience.

- Encourage interpersonal sharing between those offering service and members of the community being served. This mutual exchange enriches learning, broadens participants' worldviews, and reduces the likelihood of paternalistic attitudes.
- Challenge all family members to work side by side in meaningful roles, rather than falling into patterns where parents or other adults provide the leadership and have primary responsibilities.

Reflection: Mining Meaning from Experience

Reflection is the heart of the "learning" in service-learning, and it offers a natural link for intentional Christian formation and education. Researchers have found that people who do not reflect on service often develop negative attitudes toward serving others (*Service-Learning: Applications from the Research*). However, reflection is often the piece that is most neglected or overlooked. Leaders falsely presume that a good service experience will inevitably result in positive growth and learning. Here are some suggestions for the reflection phase:

- A basic reflection process asks three questions: What? So what? Now what? "What?" focuses on concretely remembering what was done and experienced. "So what?" shifts to interpreting the experience in light of faith, social issues, and values. "Now what?" focuses on applying the learning to life and to future service experiences.
- Use a wide range of approaches and tools for reflection and learning. These may include journaling, group discussions, research projects, developing a skit or video, writing letters to the editor about relevant social issues, and many other approaches.
- Integrate learning from service into existing educational opportunities for family members (individually and together). Having people recall their service experiences together can make otherwise abstract lessons come to life. Even those who did not participate in the experience will have the opportunity to learn and grow by hearing and processing the stories and perspectives of their fellow parishioners.

Recognition: Celebrating God's Work through God's People

The recognition phase acknowledges the service and learning that have occurred among the families involved, and worship can provide an ideal context and frame for recognition.

Recognition reinforces the value of service and sets the stage for ongoing engagement. On a theological level, recognition helps people of faith remember that their action is evidence of God's work in the world and in their lives. Some ways to enrich the recognition process include:

- Integrating themes from the service and the learning into the sacraments, prayer, music, and other elements of the liturgy.
- Having those involved in the service lead in worship for the whole congregation. Use their learning as a stimulus for growth for the whole community of faith.
- Calling everyone to build on the service-learning experience by renewing their commitment to being God's hands and feet in the world.

Putting PARR into Practice

In the abstract, this process may seem daunting. In reality, though, it provides a helpful structure that guides your efforts over time. That's easiest to see when it becomes concrete. As you read the story of one parish, you'll see the many creative ways that they put PARR into practice in family service.

When St. John of the Cross Catholic Church in Middlebury, Connecticut asked families about service opportunities, they found that families really wanted to be involved, but they didn't know how and were uncomfortable engaging in service without guidance, according to Tom Bright, who serves as the parish's justice coordinator. So the parish identified a variety of service opportunities and hosted a service fair in which families heard about different possibilities for involvement. Then families were asked to commit to one of the options. Later someone from the parish followed up with them.

The parish's goal was to move families toward greater and greater involvement and commitment. One year, families were invited to help refresh the facilities of a homeless shelter in a nearby community. For a day, families painted and cleaned. In the process, they were exposed to the need, became comfortable with being there, and had the satisfaction of seeing immediate results. The next year, the congregation organized people who had experience serving in the shelter and who were willing to be mentors for other interested families. The mentors visited with the families to prepare them for their experience, then served alongside them on their first evening in the shelter. Afterward, they reflected together about the experience. Before long, many families were comfortable and committed to serving in the shelter on a monthly basis.

Tapping the Strengths of Families

Families represent a basic strength of the faith community. When families are stronger, congregations are stronger. When Catholic families live out their mission and calling in the world, the mission of the church is enriched. By intentionally focusing on how parishes can tap into this strength, invite families to serve others, and provide opportunities and supports to make service more possible and likely, parishes have the opportunity not only to touch the lives of their parishioners, but also to more fully live out the prophet's call: "do justice and...love kindness, and...walk humbly with your God" (Micah 6:8).

Reflection Questions

1. What contribution do you believe service and acting for justice contribute to family health? to families living their faith?
2. What possibilities exist in your community for families at all life cycle stages, to engage in service and act for justice?
3. Do the service opportunities in your community employ the PARR process or something similar to it? If so, what does it look like? If not, what possibilities exist to integrate such a process?

References

Becker, Penny E. "It's Not Just a Matter of Time: How the Time Squeeze Affects Congregational Participation." *Family Ministry*, Vol 15:1. Center for Ministry Development, 2001.

Benson, Peter L. and Carolyn H Eklin. *Effective Christian Education: A National Study of Protestant Congregations*. Minneapolis Search Institute, 1990.

Blyth, Dale A., Rebecca N. Saito, and Thomas J. Berkas. "A Quantitative Study of the Impact of Service-learning Programs." In Alan S. Waterman (ed.), *Service-learning: Applications from the Research*. Mahwah, NJ: Lawrence Erlbaum, 1997.

Bright, Thomas and John Roberto. *Introduction to Action and Service Programming*. In Michael Moseley and John Roberto (eds.) *Youthworks* (rev. ed.) Naugatuck, CT: Center for Ministry Development, 1996.

Curran, Dolores. *Traits of a Healthy Family*. San Francisco: Harper and Row, 1983.

Engaging Youth in Lifelong Service. Washington, DC: Independent Sector, 2002.

Freudenberg, Ben. *The Family-Friendly Church*. Loveland, CO: Group Publishing, 1998.

Friedman, Jenny. *The Busy Family's Guide to Volunteering*. Beltsville, MD: Robins Lane Press, 2003.

Hegel, Annette and A.J. McKechnie. *Family Volunteering: The Final Report*. Ottawa, ON: Volunteer Canada, 2003.

Jalandoni, Nadine and Keith Hume. *America's Family Volunteers: Civic Participation Is a Family Matter*. Washington, DC: Independent Sector, 2001.

Kehrwald, Leif. "Families and Christian Practice." *Family Ministry*, Vol 13:4. Center for Ministry Development, 1999.

Littlepage, Laura. *Family Volunteering: An Exploratory Study of the Impact on Families*. Indianapolis: Center for Urban Policy and the Environment, 2003.

Lutheran Brotherhood Reports. "Volunteering." Press release and topline data from Lutheran Brotherhood, Minneapolis, 1997.

McGinnis, Kathleen and James McGinnis. *Parenting for Peace and Justice: Ten Years Later*. Maryknoll, NY: Orbis, 1990.

National Conference of Catholic Bishops. *Communities of Salt and Light: Reflections on the Social Mission of the Parish*. Washington, DC: United States Catholic Conference, 1994.

———. *Renewing the Vision: A Framework for Catholic Youth Ministry*. Washington, DC: United States Catholic Conference, 1997.

Price, Susan C. *The Giving Family: Raising Our Children to Help Others*. Washington, DC: Council on Foundations, 2001.

Roberto, John. "Promoting Innovative Ministry with Adolescents, Young Adults, and Families." *Family Ministry*, Vol 13:2. Center for Ministry Development, 1999.

Roehlkepartain, Eugene C. *The Teaching Church: Moving Christian Education to Center Stage*. Nashville: Abingdon, 1993.

Roehlkepartain, Eugene C. *Building Assets, Strengthening Faith: Results from a Field Test Survey of Youth and Adults in Fifteen U.S. Congregations*. Minneapolis: Search Institute, 2003.

———. "Engaging Families in Service: Rationale and Resources for Congregations." *Family Ministry*, Vol. 17:3. Center for Ministry Development, 2003.

Roehlkepartain, Eugene C., Thomas J. Bright, Beth Margolis-Rupp, and Lynn I. Nelson. *An Asset Builder's Guide to Service-Learning*. Minneapolis, MN: Search Institute, 2000.

Spaide, Deborah. *Teaching Your Kids to Care*. New York: Citadel Press, 1995.

Thoele, Mary. *Family Serve: Volunteer Opportunities for Families*. Appleton, WI: AAL QualityLife Resources, 2001.

Thompson, Marjorie J. *Family, the Forming Center: A Vision of the Role of Family in Spiritual Formation*. Nashville, TN: Upper Room, 1996.

Tropman, John E. "The Catholic ethic and the Protestant ethic." In Paul G. Schervish, et al. (eds.) *Care and Community in Modern Society: Passing on the Tradition of Service to Future Generations* San Francisco: Jossey-Bass, 1995.

Vogt, Susan. *Raising Kids Who Will Make a Difference*. Chicago: Loyola Press, 2002.

Yust, Karen-Marie. *Real Kids, Real Faith*. San Francisco: Jossey-Bass, 2004.

Service: A Family Affair

When you read biographies of great leaders, many of them tell about how much they were shaped by experiences of serving others as a family. They were moved to compassion when they saw their parents show compassion. They were challenged to stand up for truth when their parents took unpopular stands for justice. Here are some ways—big and small—that your family can become involved in serving others.

- Participate as a family in service activities sponsored by community or church groups. Talk about the experience at your family meal that evening.

- Sponsor refugees or exchange students in your home. Intentionally learn about their culture and issues in their home country.

- Make your family an "eco-team" by monitoring your own impact on the environment; then take action to reduce waste. Monitor and celebrate progress.

- Become a mentor family for a child who may not have access to healthy family models.

- Make it a family project to work together to provide—and celebrate together—birthday meals for shut-ins.

- Discuss what your family can do to respond to problems you see and hear about on the evening news or read about in the newspaper.

- Spend your Thanksgiving celebration at a local soup kitchen serving meals to the homeless.

For more specific ideas to plan service activities for your family, see *The Busy Family's Guide to Volunteering* or visit www.doinggoodtogether.org.

Chapter Ten

Tools for Responding in Ministry

Mariette Martineau

Mariette Martineau is a project specialist with the Generations of Faith project and coordinates CMD program services in Canada, including the Canadian Certificate in Youth Ministry Studies. Experienced in youth and family ministry and religious education, Mariette's ministry priority is her three children and husband.

Who's Responsible?

Family faith building impacts every leader and every ministry area in a parish. Every leader, whether volunteer or paid, has indirect or direct impact on family faith formation and practice. In *A Family Perspective in Church and Society*, the U.S. bishops wrote: "the rationale for a family perspective as a pastoral strategy is not that families are in trouble but that family life is so important in itself that it needs the ongoing support of the church. Family life is fundamental to the healthy life of the church and society" (p. 6).

Who me, you might be thinking? Yes, you! Consider the questions below to identify how your ministry area impacts family faith formation. Not every ministry is listed, but the questions apply across all ministries. Every person you minister to comes from a family of some size or shape or makeup. As Pope John Paul II said in *Familiaris Consortio*, "No plan for organized pastoral work, at any level, must ever fail to take into consideration the pastoral care of the family" (p. 70).

Consider the program or area of ministry in which you are involved. Use the following questions to elicit affirmations and challenges regarding how the program nurtures and supports the faith formation and practices of families.

Does the program or strategy…

- account for different family forms?
- account for how ethnicity impacts family life?
- have a schedule that reflects the realities of family life?
- address individual needs as well as the impact upon family life?
- improve the family's capacity to learn, pray, celebrate, serve, and build community as family?
- provide moments of silence and stillness to enable participants to better appreciate the value and impact of silence on the family path to holiness?
- build a relationship between the congregation and the family? Does the program build relationships participant to participant? participant household to participant household? the parish and civic community at large?
- help families be who they are called to be—holy and life-giving?
- provide families with resources and activities for home use?
- help families to better live out their Christian values and practice their faith at home and in the world?
- help families deal with family life cycle stage tasks and issues?

On the following pages look for the heading that pertains to your area of parish ministry. The questions under that heading will help you get a clearer focus on your response to family and household needs.

Pastor

- When presiding and preaching, do your stories and examples contain examples that the diversity of families in your parish can comprehend or relate to?
- Does your work on committees—such as pastoral council, finance, liturgy, and so on—take into consideration the family needs and cir-

cumstances of committee members? Do you see committee meetings as opportunities to enrich the lives of the members so that they might better live out their faith at home?

- Do you solicit advice from a variety of households? Do you attempt to reach out to families most in need of the parish's attention?
- When sacraments are celebrated, including the anointing of the sick, are families prepared for and involved in the celebration? Do families in your community feel affirmed in their calling to be domestic church? Is the home church as valued as the parish church?

Sacramental Preparation

- Before the celebration of the sacrament, do you prepare the whole family or just the candidate? Do you help families to learn together? to pray together? to have faith conversations and celebrate rituals? to recognize the God moments in their lives? to practice justice together?
- Does sacramental preparation provide parents with the resources and support they need to be Christian parents?

Children's Catechesis

- Is the family connected to the children's learning and activities in an intentional and direct manner? Do you know the parents of the children in your program? How do you help the adults and other siblings and family members to learn with the children?
- How do you bridge the life of your program to the life of the home, setting up the children to successfully live out their faith with support?

Youth Ministry

- Does everything you do in youth ministry ask the question, "How will this impact the home?" Are parents and guardians intentionally connected to all that takes place in youth ministry? Are opportunities provided for youth and their parents and other family members to gather together to learn, pray, and serve?
- Are parents given opportunities to meet other parents? Are support and resources provided to help parents and the adolescent households deal with their life cycle changes and needs in a healthy manner?

Adult Faith Formation

- How do adult faith formation offerings incorporate and address the needs of adults—from family life cycle needs and changes, to individual life circumstances?

- Do adult faith formation offerings happen at a variety of times and places to allow adults with different parenting schedules to attend or participate?
- What small-group options are provided to help adults learn in the context of their home?

Social Justice

- Does the parish provide opportunities for individuals and families to serve others? Does the parish use its media (bulletin, newsletters, Web site) to help families connect to service activities?
- Does the parish provide resources to help families make ethical purchases and investments, supporting retailers who are just? Does the parish provide families with connections to purchase just products like fair trade coffee and chocolate?
- Does the parish challenge families with young children to avoid violent games and TV?

Liturgy

- While respecting diocesan guidelines, how are families involved in the liturgical ministries of your parish? How welcome do families of all ages feel in your worshiping community?
- Are the needs and challenges of all families incorporated in the prayers of your community?

Pastoral Care of the Sick and Homebound

- Are family members invited to join you in prayer with the sick?
- Are resources provided for the family to deal with illness and loss?
- Are families invited to minister to the sick and shut-ins?

Who Is Family in Your Community?

Jim Merhaut states in Chapter One that "any parish that wants to minister effectively to families must develop a leadership team that appreciates the physicality of family life and holiness."

Who is "family" in your parish community? In order to effectively minister to and be inclusive of all families it is important to identify what family looks like in your parish community. Use the worksheet on the following page to list all of the family forms known in your community.

In the left-hand column list the types of families in your community. Some types include:

- Unattached adult without children
- Married without children
- Married with small children
- Single with small children
- Married with elementary-school-age children
- Single with elementary-school-age children
- Married with teenage children
- Single with teenage children
- Married with young adult children
- Single with young adult children

and so on. Imagine all of the other possibilities: widowed, multigenerational homes with elderly family members living with their children, and so on. Who makes up "family" in your parish? Does ethnicity have an impact on the naming of the family forms?

After you create the list, continue with the worksheet to estimate what percentage of the parish falls into the category of family form. For example, single with teenage children comprises what percentage of the households in your parish? Finish the worksheet by evaluating how effectively your parish ministers to, or intentionally includes, each family form.

Once the worksheet is completed, reflect on what you have discovered.

Are you surprised by the family forms that did or did not surface? Why or why not? Do you feel affirmed as you look at your evaluation of how the parish is ministering to, or intentionally including, the various families?

How do you feel challenged by the evaluation?

Making a Case for Family Faith Building

Use the following process to help your parish identify how to help families be faithful in the home.

What We Hold to be True

Every parish holds values and beliefs about family, whether they are assumed or named. What values or beliefs does your parish hold about family? To assist you in naming these values and beliefs, here are a few values held by the authors of this book. Which do you agree with? Which would you include as part of what your parish values or beliefs? What others would you add?

Who Is Family in Your Community?

With 1 being low and 5 being high, how well do you think your parish generally ministers to and intentionally includes these families?

Family Form	This family form makes up about _____% of the parish	Rating
		1 2 3 4 5
		1 2 3 4 5
		1 2 3 4 5
		1 2 3 4 5
		1 2 3 4 5
		1 2 3 4 5
		1 2 3 4 5

- "Each family must make its own path of faith formation that will lead to family holiness."
- "Families at different stages have different needs."
- "Marriage is a school of unconditional love."
- "Every day, families experience what I call 'moments of meaning' that have the potential for becoming religiously significant."
- "The daily rituals that occur in our homes happen in ways that don't look 'churchy' at all; we would never think, for example, of setting up pews in the living room. But what happens within the walls of our home is no less sacred and holy than what happens within the walls of the parish church."
- "As a family we celebrate God with us when we gather around our own kitchen tables, give thanks, and break bread. We celebrate God with us in all the seasons of our family's life by linking the stories of salvation to our own stories of birth, death, and resurrection. We celebrate God with us in concrete signs like hugs and extra cookies, Band-aids® and handing over the car keys."
- "Engaging with their families in service can be a valuable opportunity for parents to pass on key values to their children, for family members to discuss important social issues with one another, and for parishioners to make a real difference in the community while spending time with loved ones."

Where We Dare to Go

The second component of the vision framework looks into the future. It involves formulating one or more ten-year "Big Holy Audacious Goals" (BHAG), and vivid descriptions of what it will be like when the organization achieves the BHAG.

A BHAG should be so clear and compelling that it requires little or no explanation. Remember, a BHAG is a *goal*—going to the moon—not a statement. If it does not get people's juices going, then it is not a BHAG. A BHAG should fall well outside the comfort zone. People in the organization should have reason to believe they can pull it off, yet it should require heroic effort and perhaps even a little luck. A BHAG should be so bold and exciting in its own right that it would continue to stimulate progress even if the organization's leaders disappeared before it had been completed. A BHAG should be consistent with an organization's core ideology (values and purpose) (*Built to Last*, pp. 111-112).

Once your BHAGs are articulated, give each a vivid description. "Vivid description is a vibrant, engaging, and specific description of what it will be like to achieve the BHAG. Think of it as translating the vision from words into pictures, of creating an image that people can carry around in their heads" (*Built to Last* , p. 233).

What is a Big, Holy, Audacious Goal for family faith building in your parish?

Here is an example to get you started:

BHAG: Every family in our parish will read together from Scripture in their home, at least once a week.

Vivid Description: Families will look forward each week to their time to read and share Scripture together. Talking about Scripture will feel as comfortable as talking about a favorite TV program or sports team. The bibles in each home will not look dusty but used. Family members will be asking questions about Scripture in faith formation sessions and at other contact points they have with the parish.

Our BHAG:

Vivid Description:

Creating Alignment

To insure that your day-to-day activity actually works toward implementing your BHAGs, you must create alignment in all you do. This means two things: creating new strategies that preserve your core values and beliefs and stimulate progress, and eliminating activity that drives you away from your envisioned future. Give serious consideration to these questions:

- What can we *add* to our ministry to better preserve our core values and core purpose and stimulate progress? Make specific recommendations for action.

- What should we *eliminate* from our ministry that's currently driving us away from our core values and core purpose and/or blocking our progress? Make specific recommendations for action.
- What do we need to *create* in order to implement our BHAGs (new alignments: programs, activities, procedures, etc.)?

Making Family Faith Building a Reality

Each parish has different strengths, weaknesses, resources, and visions. Each parish must discern its best possible response at this time, not simply doing what is comfortable, but acting with integrity to serve the families in its community. Here are three ways a parish can strengthen its support for family faith formation and practice.

1. Deepen Existing Contact with Families

There are many potential points of contact between the parish and the family. These points can be the start of positive faith building through support and helpful resources. Review the points of contact listed below. Which ones are currently being used to assist families in faith building? Are there some points that can be better utilized for offering resources, support, and relationship building? For example:

- parish registration,
- Sunday Eucharist,
- other worship and sacramental celebrations,
- parish bulletins, newsletters, or Web sites,
- parish social events,
- parish school events,
- parish service events.

What is one immediate change or adjustment your parish can make? What is one long-term goal?

2. Provide Follow-Up Options

If parishes across Canada and the United States were to be surveyed about how well they follow up programs and celebrations, such as sacramental preparation, many would say they have little in place once the sacrament or event has been celebrated. A child is baptized, an adult is welcomed through the RCIA process, a young couple is married—and very little is intentionally offered by our parishes to build upon those experiences for the participants and their families.

Which of the following options does your parish do for follow-up? Which options might you consider doing?

- Provide informal gatherings for participants to gather to share their experience and to reflect on the impact of that experience in their lives.
- Offer resources to continue the praying, learning, ritualizing, relationship building, and serving at home or in small groups. Resources can include prayers, table rituals, contemporary movies to discuss, and so on.
- Send a newsletter to connect participants to ongoing learning and other parish events that might be of interest to them. Send an email each day or each week with a brief prayer in it.
- Use the parish Web site to provide daily reflections or resources such as parenting courses and family events.
- Provide access to independent learning materials, such as books, videos, and magazine articles. Host a book fair to give households access to resources they may not be familiar with.
- Provide physical reminders of the experience, such as items for the home altar or prayer area.
- Create prayer partners and prayer circles.
- Provide ritual calendars and prayer books.
- Provide monthly a scheduled justice activity for families to engage in—one in which they are able to join even if they cannot commit on a regular basis.
- Provide journals for participants to record their reflections in, providing them with a reflection process as well as questions to ponder.

What is one immediate change or adjustment your parish can make? What is one long-term goal?

3. Implementing New Programs

After assessing its current programs, existing contact points, and follow-up options, a parish may realize that it may be time to implement a new program to support faith formation in the home. Some options to consider include:

Family Retreats and Camps. Some parishes and dioceses have the tradition of an annual family retreat or camp. Families of all ages and makeup are invited together for a weekend or week. A blend of learning, community building, and prayer are offered along with some free time to simply be together.

Helpful resources

- The CFL Family Retreat Center, lay-owned and operated in the Marianist tradition, offers fun and faith-filled family empowerment retreats emphasizing affirmation, communication skills, reconciliation, and commitment. Ed DeBerri, Director, 2006 Wicker St., North Topsail Beach, NC 28460, 910-328-1584, www.christianfamilyliving.org.
- The Story of Us Family Retreat, Family Life Office, Archdiocese of Galveston-Houston, 2403 Holcombe Blvd., Houston, TX 77201-2023, 713-741-8730, www.diogh.org/FamilyLife/index.htm.
- Family Guggenheim, Diocese of Ogdensburg Family Retreat Program, 100 Elizabeth St., P.O. Box 369, Ogdensburg, NY 13669, 315-393-2920, http://dioogdensburg.org/family-life/.
- Spirit of Life Summer Camp, Spirit of Life Church, P.O. Box 247, Mandan, ND 58554, 701-663-1660.
- Emmaus Family Weekends, Family Life Office, Diocese of Altoona-Johnstown, 5379 Portage St., Lilly, PA 15938, 814-886-5551, www.ajdiocese.org/min/fl.html.

Intergenerational Learning Programs. Many parishes are realizing how much impact intergenerational learning programs can have on the families in their community. The Generations of Faith approach involves the whole family (from children through grandparents) in parish faith formation and equips parents with the knowledge and skills needed for sharing faith at home. Through intergenerational catechetical programs, families have the opportunity to learn together, often for the first time. Parents and grandparents are engaged in the process of learning and sharing faith with the children, while building their knowledge and confidence.

At each intergenerational catechetical program, families and individuals receive a home kit that extends and expands their learning from the parish catechetical program into their home life. It provides activities and resources to help families celebrate traditions and rituals, continue their learning, pray together, serve others and work for justice, and enrich their relationships and family life.

Helpful resources

- *People of Faith: Generations Learning Together.* Orlando: Harcourt Religion Publishers 2005-2008. The *People of Faith* series includes six intergenerational parish program manuals with six sessions per manual and forty-eight household magazines.

- Martineau, Mariette. *People of Faith Organizer's Manual*. Orlando: Harcourt Religion Publishers, 2005.
- Roberto, John and Mariette Martineau. *Generations of Faith Resource Manual: Lifelong Faith Formation for the Whole Parish Community*. New London, CT: Twenty-Third Publications, 2005.
- Roberto, John. *Becoming a Church of Lifelong Followers: The Generations of Faith Sourcebook*. New London, CT: Twenty-Third Publications, 2006.

Small Christian Neighborhood or *Interest-based Communities*. Small Christian communities or neighborhood cell groups have been proven effective in supporting and nurturing the faith of families.

Helpful resources

- Christian Family Movement (CFM) is a national network of parish/neighborhood small groups of families. Parents meet regularly in one another's homes. Through the use of CFM resources and the dynamics of small group interaction, Christian values are reinforced and families are encouraged to reach out in action to support others. CFM USA National Office, P.O. Box 925, Evansville, IN 47706-0925, 812-962-5508, www.cfm.org.
- *Faith Sharing for Small Church Communities: Questions and Commentaries on the Sunday Readings*, edited by Rev. Arthur Baranowski and the National Alliance for Parishes Restructuring into Communities. St. Anthony Messenger Press, 1615 Republic Street, Cincinnati, OH 45210, 513-241-5615, www.americancatholic.org.

Family Service and Justice Education. More service agencies are providing opportunities for families to serve together. Do some research on the possibilities in your area. Encourage family participation in national programs such as Operation Rice Bowl and Make Poverty History.

Helpful resources

- *People of Faith: Generations Learning Together*, "Acting For Justice" parish manual and family magazines. Orlando: Harcourt Religion Publishers, 2005, www.harcourtreligion.com.
- *Institute for Peace and Justice, Parenting for Peace and Justice Network*, and *Families Against Violence Advocacy Network*. An independent,

interfaith, nonprofit organization that creates resources, provides learning experiences, and advocates publicly for alternatives to violence and injustice at the individual, family, community, institutional, and global levels. Contact them at 4144 Lindell Boulevard #408, St. Louis, MO 63108, 314-533-4445, www.ipj-ppj.org.

- Vogt, Susan. *Raising Kids Who Will Make a Difference.* Loyola Press.
- Vogt, Susan. *Just Family Nights: Activities to Keep Your Family Together in a World That Is Falling Apart.* Faith Quest, 1994.

Monthly "Home" or Family Nights. Challenge families to have a monthly home night and provide them with ideas. Home activities might include preparing a favorite meal together, viewing a movie (with discussion options), holding a board game night, having a closet sorting to see who can gather the most items to give away to those in need, and so on. Sometimes we miss great things in our communities like parks, community festivals, and such. Point out monthly event options to the households in your community.

Helpful resources

- *People of Faith: Generations Learning Together* family magazines. Orlando: Harcourt Religion Publishers, 2005.
- *At Home with Our Faith.* This family spirituality newsletter provides ideas and resources to help pass on a living faith. Mary Lynn Hendricksen and Cathy O'Connell-Cahill (eds.), www.homefaith.com.
- *The Word Among Us: Family Edition* features a sixteen-page insert with articles on family life. In addition, subscribers get all the content of *The Word Among Us*, including daily meditations based on the Mass readings, articles on the saints, and personal stories of faith. 800-775-9673, www.wau.org.

Gathered Programs or Support Groups for Specific Family Life Cycle Needs. Provide opportunities for parents to gather for ideas, support, and community time. Most parents desire to hear that their home is "normal" and to receive from one another, and experts, a few parenting pointers and insights. Sometimes a local coffee shop or lounge is more inviting than a parish meeting room.

Helpful resources

- McGrath, Tom. *Raising Faith-Filled Kids: Ordinary Opportunities to Nurture Spirituality at Home.* Loyola Press.

- Pettycrew, Eileen. *Growing Up Girl: Sharing Your Heart With Your Mom*. Saint Mary's Press.
- Brennan, Tina. *Sacred Gifts: Extraordinary Lessons from My Ordinary Teens*. Saint Mary's Press.
- Pedersen, Mary Jo, et al. *More Than Meets the Eye: Finding God in the Creases and Folds of Family Life*. Saint Mary's Press.

Tables for Two. This idea originated as an opportunity for couples or a parent and child to spend time together as a pair. In its original format, the gathering begins with a simple prayer service, followed by the serving of a five-course meal. With each course of the meal a question is provided for the pair to discuss. The meal closes with prayer, and the pair is given some resources to continue the sharing at home.

From the program ideas above, what is one immediate change or adjustment your parish can make? What is one long-term goal?

Milestone Celebrations

For families to remember how sacred their lives are, it is helpful to mark some of their rites of passage. Milestones such as a child starting school, receiving a driver's license, moving away from home, and so on, can be marked at a parish celebration or gathering.

Use the worksheet on the next page to assess your parish's efforts at supporting a family's faith formation leading up to a sacramental or milestone event, and following up afterward. Helpful resources:

- *Across the Generations: Incorporating All Ages in Ministry*, Augsburg Fortress, (800) 328-4648, www.augsburgfortress.org.
- *Kitchen Table Gospel*. This intergenerational resource deals only with the Liturgical Year, gathering parish families four times a year for seasonal rallies. It offers a variety of ideas for families with children of all ages, www.mhschool.com/benziger.

Faith Formation through the Family Life Cycle

Reviewing Our Community's Response

- In what ways does our parish prepare families or households to engage in this sacrament or rite of passage?
- How does our parish continue to support and nurture faith after this sacrament or rite of passage has been celebrated?

Preparation	Sacrament or Rite of Passage	Continued Support
	Leaving Home	
	First Career/Job	
	Engagement	
	Marriage	
	Blessing of New Home	
	Birth or Adoption	

Preparation	Sacrament or Rite of Passage	Continued Support
	Baptism	
	Beginning School	
	First Reconciliation	
	First Eucharist	
	Confirmation	
	Receipt of Driver's License	
	Graduation from High School	
	Retirement	
	Transition into Care	
	Sacrament of Anointing	
	Rite of Funerals	

Connecting Life and Faith: Teaching the Four-Step Process

Chapter Five describes a four-step process designed to help families reflect upon moments of meaning in their lives, and mine those moments for their faith implications. Consider the following strategies for teaching the process to families.

Integrate It into Currently Existing Programs. Teach the four-step process in sacramental preparation programs, program parent evenings, and teach it to children and youth with resources to carry it home to share with their family. Invite participants to name a moment of meaning that they have shared, and guide them through the process.

Take-home Resources. Provide the four-step process in a user-friendly format. Print it in bookmark size or on a refrigerator magnet. Create symbols for each step so that families can use them in the process. Provide families with examples, like those provided in Chapter Five.

Publish It. Invite families to submit some of their moment-of-meaning reflections to the parish Web site or bulletin. Invite sharing at follow-up meetings, and so on.

Gathered Event that Highlights the Process. Host a memory-sharing event; call it, "We Remember, We Celebrate, We Believe." Invite families to bring scrapbooks with them. Guide them through the four-step process using a memory of their choosing. Invite them to work together and then to share their reflection with another family. This can be for families whose children are about to start school, or for families whose children are about to graduate from high school and are preparing to leave home, and so on.

Host an Intergenerational Learning Event in the Easter Season and connect the events to the Sunday that has the Walk to Emmaus story as the gospel (Luke 24:13–35). Help participants to learn the four-step process by connecting it to the Emmaus story.

References

A Family Perspective in Church and Society. United States Conference of Catholic Bishops' Committee on Marriage and Family. Washington, DC: USCCB Publishing, 1998.

Collins, James C. and Jerry I. Porras. *Built To Last: Successful Habits of Visionary Companies.* New York: Harper Collins, 1997.

Pope John Paul II. *Familiaris Consortio.* Vatican City: Libreria Editrice Vaticana, 1981.

Worksheet

Connecting Life and Faith

A moment of meaning has just occurred.

Awareness. Stop! Look! Listen!
Someone recognizes that the family is having a moment of meaning.
Someone points it out to everyone else so that all are aware.

Acknowledge It!
As a whole, the family acknowledges the presence of the Spirit
in their midst. The routine of ordinary life is disrupted
to make room to embrace the new experience.

Connect to the Sacred.
The family either chooses to pursue it further, or to let it go.
Questions to pursue:
• How does our story connect to the Jesus story?
• How do we pray about this encounter,
or how does this encounter change our prayer?
• Who are the wisdom people with whom we should connect?
• How does this encounter intersect with the life of
our faith community and our religious practice?

So What?
What difference has this experience made in our lives? What memory
have we created? How will we revisit it? What have we learned?
How will it change our behavior?

Final Note

It's a simple fact: parents are the primary educators in the faith. It is perhaps more important for parish leaders to recognize this fact than it is for parents to do so. Parents will always have more influence on the faith journeys of their children. But only when parish leaders fully recognize and accept this fact will genuine partnership between the church of the parish and the church of the home become possible.

Just as the parish is challenged to be a healthy faith formation program for all parishioners, so too the family is challenged to be a faith formation system for all members, not just children. Like the parish, the home is called to be a school of discipleship. Yet we must always remember that the ecclesial nature of the home does not and should not mimic the parish. The home must become a school for the most basic of human activity: rising, bathing, eating, cleaning up, relaxing, dying, grieving, embracing…and how the values of the Kingdom of God are inculcated in these, the most mundane activities.

Families can and should learn a great deal from the parish about forming one another in faith through worship, education, prayer, and service. Yet parishes can and should learn a great deal from families about how to be a community of love and life.